History **&** Guide

MUSWELL HILL

Ken Gay

History & Guide

MUSWELL HILL

Ken Gay

The History Press

First published in 2002 by Tempus Publishing

Reprinted 2010 by
The History Press
The Mill, Brimscombe Port,
Stroud, Gloucestershire, GL5 2QG
www.thehistorypress.co.uk

Reprinted 2012

British Library Cataloguing in Publication Data.
A catalogue record for this book is available from the British Library.

ISBN 978 0 7524 2604 4

Typesetting and origination by
Tempus Publishing Limited
Printed in Great Britain.

Contents

PREFACE & ACKNOWLEDGEMENTS

The presence of well-known actors, television presenters and media people as residents has drawn increasing attention in recent years to Muswell Hill, and helped make the price of its period Edwardian family houses rise even further, with the suburb regularly featuring in the property pages of national newspapers. The hundred-year-old suburb of London bears all this with grace, having from the start been seen as a special hilltop place with good local shops and many surrounding open spaces, and always drawing to it people who appreciated its charms. This history tries to show that Muswell Hill, even in its under-populated past had a natural beauty which drew widespread praise, and a certain isolation from the stress of city life that made it an ideal retreat and place to live. In its pages I have tried to outline how it evolved from hamlet to desirable London suburb.

As with my previous local history books I have been helped and sustained by my colleagues in Hornsey Historical Society and once again I must thank them for their support. When I joined the society in 1979 I had no idea how it would soon immerse me in its activities and lead me to devote a great portion of my life to studying local history. The result has been over two decades of comradeship and pleasure, helping to bring to public attention the history of the local environment and to conserve the best of its features.

I would like to acknowledge and thank all those who helped me with illustrations for the book, including those at Bruce Castle who look after the archives of the London Borough of Haringey, particularly Deborah Hedgecock and Rita Reed. I owe a special debt to Hugh Garnsworthy who kindly loaned me his large collection of historic postcards on which I have freely drawn. I also have to thank Anthony Edmondson and John Farr for their family photo of James Edmondson.

CHAPTER 1
Early Times

Muswell Hill is a hilltop suburb nearly six miles north of London. Built up from 1896, mainly by two developers, it has a homogenity of Edwardian style rarely seen elsewhere. Its arrival provided the middle classes with substantial family homes set in tree-lined avenues, with distinctive terraced shopping parades. A hundred or so years later the suburb remains virtually unaltered except for a few later buildings and the changes forced upon it by mass motorized traffic. It retains its appeal as a fine place to live.

Memories of the small Middlesex village replaced by the Edwardian suburb have gone, along with recollections of the private estates with detached houses which for centuries characterized the area. The occupiers had successfully resisted urban development till the very end of the nineteenth century, despite the building up in the second half of the Victorian era of most of the rest of Hornsey, the ancient parish in which Muswell Hill was set. So what is the history of the place as a settlement?

One must look first at the geographical factors that helped to determine its history. The key fact about Muswell Hill is its height and its remoteness. If you stand in Muswell Hill Broadway and look down the steep Hillfield Park you see a grand vista of the Thames Valley covered

View from Hillfield Park.

View from the top of Muswell Hill.

with buildings; these days you get your bearings from the tall towers of Canary Wharf. Then there is the Lea Valley, which you can see from the top of Muswell Hill, just beyond the roundabout. Or even better, you can see this eastward view from the bend in Alexandra Park Road by St Andrew's church; in the distance are the green Essex slopes on the far side of the valley, leading up to Epping Forest on the distant ridge.

In any town, let alone a great city like London, there is something comforting in looking across an urban landscape to see green fields beyond. It is the supreme trick of the best of the suburbs to offer urban delights and rural prospects, and Muswell Hill does this. On its south side it is bounded by ancient Highgate and Queen's Woods, and then by the many acres of Crouch End Playing Fields. On the east side are the 200 acres of Alexandra Park, on the north the remnants of Coldfall Woods.

It was this recipe of hilltop views and surviving greenery that, over the centuries, attracted more comfortably-off Londoners to establish country estates here – a geographical prospect that determined its land use. These geographical factors still exist today, making the Edwardian suburb distinctive and satisfying for those that live there.

Muswell Hill is high because it stands at the edge of a plateau formed by glacial deposits from the last Ice Age. Its hilly nature and the streams running from it for a long time deterred the building of roads, and its heavy clay soil, suitable for the growth of trees and woods, deterred the development of arable farming to any large extent. So the larger agricultural populations that arable farming needs did not develop here on any great scale. Instead, when clearances took place it was for pasture and dairy farming. Animals were grazed and hay grown. The numbers who lived there were small, centering around the needs of the owners and occupants of the small estates and farms that came to occupy the landscape. Common land and waste remained at its heart.

When did settlement begin? Unfortunately we know little about the Neolithic, Bronze- and Iron-Age peoples who might have been here. Across the British Isles work by archaeologists year by year reveals more and more about these early peoples, finding their skeletons and cemeteries, the foundations of their homes and their artefacts. However, little has been uncovered in this now built-up area. A Bronze-Age flint dagger was found in the nineteenth century but the site of the discovery was not recorded. So we do not know whether the first paths along this plateau and the ridge leading to Hampstead, known as the Northern Heights, were made by early peoples, who may have sheltered in the woods that covered the high land.

We know more about the Romans who in AD 43 landed on the south coast of the island and proceeded to conquer the country. In the Lea valley, three miles away from the ridge on which the Muswell Hill suburb now stands, they drove a road north – a major road that exists as a route to this day. Known later as Ermine Street, part of it was to become Tottenham High Road. In contrast to hilly and neglected Muswell Hill this major route was over the centuries to lead to roadside settlement. By the early eighteenth century Daniel Defoe is describing Tottenham as an urban village, strung along the road; its legacy is a wealth of neglected Georgian houses lining the northern part of Tottenham High Road. Without the major road Muswell Hill remained a hilly wooded backwater.

Muswell Hill and the surrounding area has so far yielded no evidence of Roman farms or villas, though the poor soil, the hills and the woods, are probably the reason for their absence. But Romans, or Romanized Britons, were here. In Highgate Woods the remains of a seasonal Roman pottery have been excavated. A mile or so away in Cranley Gardens a buried Roman pot was found in a garden in 1928; it contained 694 coins from around AD 209, a bronze ring and a silver spoon, now in the British Museum. In 1970 two pots, possibly dating from the first century AD, were found just beyond Highgate woods in Southwood Lawn Road. Other scattered Roman coins, such as the fourth-century coin of Constantine the Great, found in 1927 in Barrenger Road, Muswell Hill, remind us of a Roman presence. How the coins came to be buried or lost is unknown, likewise by what Roman road or route the pottery products were transported to market.

Local history more properly begins after the Roman forces left in the fifth century AD with the next invasion of settlers. People migrated to these islands from the northern part of Europe – an element of the many migrations of tribes that took place in this early medieval period to determine the way Europe was peopled. Those that came to Britain, and

were responsible for the name 'England', became known generally as the Anglo-Saxons – Angles, Saxons and Jutes, migrating Germanic tribes who came to dominate the south. Many of the place names in Middlesex, Essex and Hertfordshire derive from these settlers. Not only did they clear land to farm, they gave their names to places, developed road systems, established land-ownership boundaries and developed kingdoms and governmental systems, including the concept of the manor. When the pagan peoples were converted to Christianity they established churches, sometimes on former sites of pagan worship, and were to lay the foundations for a later system of parishes that would mainly be developed across the country after the Norman Conquest of 1066. The basic shaping of local settlement seems to emerge from this era, to be consolidated later by the Normans. Boundaries that were established in this long-ago period, and other legacies including the definition of land ownership, still affect us today.

Archaeological work reveals more each year about these Saxon peoples, whose arrival and development of the Christian church in this country were written about as long ago as 731 by the Wearmouth-based monk Bede in his famous Historia Ecclesiastic Gentis Anglorum. Written in Latin, the language of the Romans, this 'Ecclesiastical History of the English Nation' was translated into Old English by Alfred the Great, the greatest of the Saxon kings.

Old English is the term we now use to describe the language of the Germanic tribes, as this formed the basis of the English language which, as we have seen, has developed over the centuries to become the language most used across the globe, its tribal origins ending in a great instrument of communication for all peoples.

Saxon immigration would have been by boat across the North Sea and then probably by river valley or river to penetrate the forests and to create farmsteads and settlements which they named. Heringes-hege (with the 'g's pronounced as 'y's) was the place name of most importance to our locality. Said by historian Dr S.J. Madge to mean the enclosure of Haering or Hering's people it became the root of many different spellings of our main local place name; Dr Madge published an account of about 160 variants which he found in medieval and later documents. 'Harringeie', as it was sometimes spelt by Tudor times, became corrupted into 'Harnsey' or 'Hornsey'. By the eighteenth century Hornsey was established as the most-used version. When in 1965 the Borough of Hornsey was merged with the Borough of Wood Green and the Borough of Tottenham to form one of the new enlarged outer London boroughs the name given to the new local authority was Haringey.

Where was this early Saxon enclosure which gave its name to our area? One possibility is near where the parish church of St Mary, Hornsey, was later built, the surviving fifteenth-century tower of which still stands in Hornsey High Street. This is located in the north-east corner of a parish that once occupied about four square miles (to include Muswell Hill) and which may originally have had the same boundaries as Hornsey manor. It was the village of Hornsey, which may have developed out of the original Saxon settlement place, which was to give its name to the parish and manor.

The date when this manor was established is not known but the Bishop of London was lord of the manor before and after the Norman Conquest. The manor was not listed separately in the Domesday Book in 1086 because it was part of the Bishop's larger manor of Stepney. Ownership of local land by the Church was to continue down the centuries, passing to the Ecclesiastical Commissioners and then the Church Commissioners.

Whether the Saxon settlers had created a manor before the establishment of a bishopric for London we do not know. The bishopric came only after the conversion of the southern pagan tribes to Christianity. The Celtic west, particularly Ireland, was Christian by the early sixth century but in the south conversion began with the arrival in AD 597 on the Kent coast of (St) Augustine and his 40-strong mission. Sent by Pope Gregory, Augustine's success depended upon the conversion of local kings in a divided island of separate kingdoms with small populations. The first king he approached, according to Bede, was Ethelbert, who allowed Augustine to lodge in Canterbury.

Gradually Christianity came to be the religion practised and a system of Church government evolved, with pastoral work among local communities and the provision of baptism, wedding and burial rites. The Church was allowed by later kings, when a more unified kingdom had been established, to set up a system of taxation known as tithes to pay for the expense of the church and its incumbent. Defined parishes gradually emerged, sometimes related to existing manorial boundaries, as seems to have been the case at Hornsey. The first record of the parish church of St Mary is in 1291 when a survey was undertaken of English churches for ecclesiastical taxation purposes by the Pope. The first record of a priest and a rectory is 1302, the living being in the gift of the Bishop of London. St Mary's in Hornsey village was to be the place of worship for residents of Muswell Hill.

Taken over by the Normans and developed by them, the manorial system gave the lord of the manor ownership of the land, under the monarch. There were various types of tenure, rights and obligations. Customs were enforced and tenure endorsed by a Court Baron, and conduct and jurisdiction by a Court Leet. These manorial courts ran local affairs for centuries. Change was to come in the Tudor period when responsibility for operating new poor laws was given to parishes. The

local church vestry gradually became the centre of local government, though the manorial courts continued to operate for some time. Muswell Hill was therefore ultimately to be controlled, and taxed, by Hornsey parish.

Muswell Hill was to have two place names. The first was 'Pinnsknoll'. Dr Madge sees this as a difficult name to interpret but its meaning was probably 'Pinn's knoll, or summit, from the personal name of Pinn'. It must be emphasised that the name was applied to the hill, not to the road that ran up it, or to any settlement. The records for the manor of Hornsey show that this name was still in use in the seventeenth century. Madge argues however that during the fifteenth and sixteenth centuries the alternative name of Muswell Hill became fixed.

The name Muswell Hill derives not only from the actual hill but also from springs or wells. The location of these is about where No. 40 Muswell Road (the turning off Colney Hatch Lane) has been built. A plaque on the house names this as the spot. From these springs issued the Muswell stream which runs eastwards downhill towards the Lea (now culverted). The first element of the word Muswell came from the Old English word meos meaning moss and the second element from the Old English mielle meaning well, fountain or spring, according to Dr Madge. The name can thus be taken to mean 'the hill of the mossy spring'. These wells were to become important in the medieval history of Muswell Hill. In later centuries various spellings were used such as 'Mussell Hill' in 1631 and 'Muscle Hill' in 1746. Standardization of spelling was to take a long time to establish in the days of widespread illiteracy.

Road systems developed in the area over the centuries, connecting the small local settlements which emerged. Routes connected Hornsey village and Crouch End and beyond, and other routes led to Muswell Hill and Highgate. These were country tracks along which livestock could be driven and journeys made, often through mud on foot or by cart. The dominating interest was connection with London.

I have not so far mentioned London but the city, with its overpowering demands for food, labour and countryside locations, greatly influenced the area around it, its hinterland. Geography again influences history. It was because the river Thames was a good natural harbour where the sea tide turned that London grew. First established by the Romans as Londinium, the settlement was developed on two gravel hills amongst the shallows and marshes of the wide river. As the centuries passed, more merchants began to trade from here, first to the Baltic, the Rhine and the Mediterranean and then further afield, for the harbour and the city were at a favourable nodal point on the globe for trade and ships were to sail from there to the Far East and to the Americas, and eventually to Australia. It was to be one of the great ports in the history of the western world. Merchants were able to grow very rich, and it was this feature that was the basis of London's importance. As a great city it drew to it central government and it became the country's capital. It became the country's greatest centre for manufacture, hosting many trades. Muswell Hill's history was to reflect the nearness of this great city and the demands of Londoners. Eventually it was to become one of its suburbs.

The main route that connected Muswell Hill to London in the early medieval period came through Crouch End, along what is now called Park Road, up the steep Muswell Hill and then along Colney Hatch Lane to Whetstone and the north. Apparently it was not a good road, deep in mud in winter and rutted in summer. Streams drained on to it from the higher ground – even in the 1960s Park Road was flooded near the foot of Muswell Hill. According to John Norden, writing in his *Speculum Britanniae*, published in 1539, this road was so bad that another route developed out of Holloway up Highgate Hill to proceed towards Barnet as the Great North Road.

This development of a new road did not occur until the Bishop of London gave permission for a road across his large hunting park, which stretched from Kenwood to the edge of Muswell Hill. The bishop was charging a toll by 1319 and as the road took more travellers Highgate grew as a settlement. The name Highgate is earlier than the toll and derives from Heygate or Heghgate (from *haia* – a hedge and *gata* – a road), meaning 'the road through the hedge' (surrounding the bishop's park). Highgate was to be situated on the parish boundary between Hornsey and St Pancras, the dividing line running down the High Street. Today it is the boundary between Haringey and Camden, the outer London boroughs created in 1965 to supplant their smaller predecessors.

Highgate grew as the road became important for trade with London, especially as a route whereby drovers could bring livestock to London's markets. Situated on a healthy hilltop it became a place for aristocratic residents to enjoy country air in out-of-town mansions. Alehouses were also built to serve the needs of travellers. A survey of licensed victuallers in 1552 showed that Highgate had five compared with three for Hornsey and only one for Muswell Hill.

The Muswell Hill alehouse is assumed to be the Green Man (now renamed) at the top of Muswell Hill; there travellers would pause after the climb. It was at a road junction, for at the top of the hill another road went south to Highgate. Appropriately this was named Southwood Lane, and the section beyond the 1812 Archway Road retains this name. It was in the nineteenth century that part of the road was renamed Muswell Hill Road. In the mid-twentieth century the last part of this was renamed again as Muswell Hill Broadway, but the route itself may well go back to before the Norman Conquest. For it must be remembered that in many

The Old Green Man. Muswell Hill 1864.

The Green Man in 1864.

cases roads last far longer than buildings and settlements. So too do place names, though thet are often modified as language changes. Boundaries of land ownership too are fairly immutable. These three elements are the core of local history.

The junction of the road up Muswell Hill and the one to the south, to Highgate, is now the site of the roundabout; Queen's Avenue and Duke's Avenue, which also now join at this junction, date only from 1897 and 1900 respectively. One other earlier road, in two sections, is now called Fortis Green Road and Fortis Green; this road led to East Finchley, which grew up where the new road from Highgate exited from the Bishop's hunting park. Where Fortis Green Road turns east to become Fortis Green another ancient road joins, now called Tetherdown but previously known as Tatterdown. This led to Coppett's Farm and to the valley of the Bounds Green Brook, now the route of the North Circular Road. The name Fortis Green is obscure in origin, according to the English Place Name Society. It is recorded in Hornsey manorial court rolls in 1613 as Fortessegreene. In his 1754 map of Middlesex John Roque labels it Forty Green but the 1816 Enclosure Award calls it Fortis Green. Fortis House was the name of an important Muswell Hill property in Fortis Green Road.

For centuries these roads led through undeveloped lands, for even in Tudor times much of Hornsey parish (including Muswell Hill) was wooded with commons and wastes. Only gradually was it taken over for farming and to establish estates. For example, ascending Muswell Hill to its summit the land on the left-hand side was known as Muswell Hill Common; it was bounded on the far side by a route known today as St James' Lane. In the hollow at the foot of this lane a small settlement was to develop. This community became known as the old village, and was still referred to as such by local inhabitants in the late twentieth century. The cottages provided homes for the workers needed by the estate occupants and farmers, including tradespeople. Muswell Hill Common was parcelled out into private ownership under the 1816 Enclosure Award under act of Parliament but the land still remained largely open until the end of the nineteenth century.

Another common, known as Hornsey Common, lay on the west side of Tetherdown, merging with Coldfall Wood, which was once much larger in size. To the south the wood stretched down to Fortis Green and to the north it merged with Finchley Common. This was a vast tract of wood and waste which travellers had to traverse on their journey to and from London on the north road. In the eighteenth century Finchley Common became an ideal location for highwaymen and robbers.

The first known development of this land of wood and waste at Muswell Hill occurred in the twelfth century, and it provides us with the first written record of the use of the local name. The twelfth century was, in Europe, a period when religious orders and houses were being founded. Newly established on the outskirts of London at Clerkenwell was the priory of St Mary. This was a house of Augustinian Canonesses, founded in around 1145 by Jordan de Bricet, who also established the nearby house of Knights Hospitallers of St John of Jerusalem. Within fifty years of its foundation this priory had widespread possessions in the south of England.

Richard de Belmeis, bishop of London from 1152 until his death in 1161, granted the priory land at Muswell Hill. The original charter was probably made in 1152 – it is mentioned soon afterwards in a surviving confirmatory charter of Archbishop Theobald. In his book entitled *The Early Records of Harringay alias Hornsey*, Dr S.J. Madge reproduces a photograph of this charter and provides a transcript of the Latin text:

'Confirmation by Theobaldus, Archbishop of Canterbury, to Cristiana, prioress and the nuns of St Mary's Priory, Clerkenwell, of grants of land at Muswell and Newington given by Richard, Bishop of London, Jordan (Briset) and Bertrand fil. Theodori, and of tithes given by Henry de Essex.

'Theobald by the grace of God Archbishop of Canterbury primate of all England legate of the Apostolic seat To all the

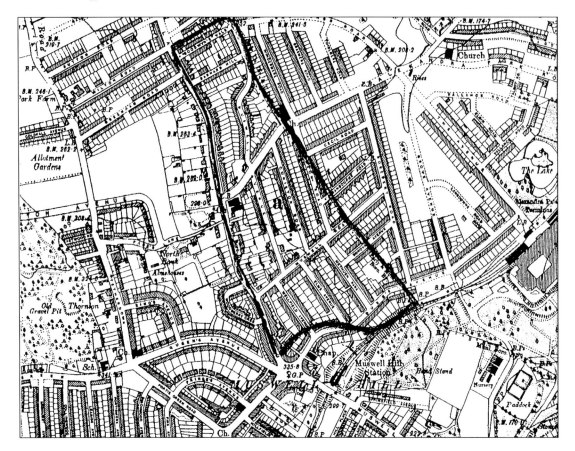

Clerkenwell Detached boundaries marked on a 1920 OS map.

faithful of holy mother church Greeting...now we that we have hearkened to the just supplications of Cristiana the prioress and other holy ones of the church of Blessed Mary of Clerkenewell and those things which justly and canonically according to the tenor of the charter of our venerable brother Richard, bishop of London they now possess...to wit, these possessions, the land of Mosewelle...and eighty acres at Neuton [Newington].'

The Muswell Hill land lay on the east side of Colney Hatch Lane and had probably been undeveloped roadside manorial land in the gift of the bishop of London when his grant was made. It was over sixty-four acres in extent. On today's map it can be said to have been between Goodwyns Vale in the north and Duke's Avenue in the south. To the east it reached to the boundary between the parishes of Hornsey and Tottenham. This boundary can be identified today by the metal markers which still survive, erected in 1934 to mark the boundary between Hornsey Borough and Wood Green Borough (formerly a part of Tottenham parish, it was made a borough at this time).

Land in Tottenham manor was also granted to the Augustinian Canonesses of St Mary at Clerkenwell. Given between 1165 and 1176 this grant probably abutted the Muswell Hill property for it consisted of some 140 acres in the 'hanger' of Tottenham. A hanger is a wood growing on a steep hillside and this description can be applied to the hill on which Alexandra Palace was to be built in the nineteenth century. This site was occupied by Tottenham Wood until the middle of the eighteenth century.

The grant to the nuns of manorial land at Muswell Hill marks the emergence of the place into recorded history. The nuns developed the land as a farm. This can be seen as an early example of London's hinterland being used for food production by those living in or near the capital. More interestingly, the wells situated on the nuns' land gained a reputation for being holy and effecting cures for diseases. In a medieval equivalent to Lourdes, the place drew pilgrims seeking cure for their diseases. But in a comparatively little-populated country with no transport system, the numbers coming would have been small. The story is told by John Norden in his treatise published in 1539, nearly four hundred years after the events supposedly took place:

> 'At Muswell Hill, called also Pinsenell Hill, there was a Chapel here sometime bearing the name of Our Ladie of Muswell, where now Alderman Roe hath erected a proper house, for there is on the hill a spring of faire water, which is nowe within the compasse of the house. There was sometime an image of the ladie of Muswell, whereunto was a continuall resort, in the way of pilgrimage, growing as (though I take it) fabulously reported, in respect of a great cure which was performed by this water, upon a king of Scots, who being strangely diseased, was by some divine intelligence advised to take the water of a well in England called Muswell, which after a long scrutation, and inquisition, this well was found and performed the cure; absolutely to denie the cure I dare not, for that the high God hath given virtue unto waters, to heal infirmities, as may appear by the cure of Naaman the leper.'

Norden does not give the king's name, but he was identified by local historian Dr Draper as Malcolm IV who ruled from 1153 to 1165, dying at the age of twenty-four. Tottenham manor was in the possession of the Scottish royal house for a period (its current name, Bruce Castle, is a reference to this) and Malcolm had granted the Tottenham hanger lands to Robert of Northampton on condition that he left them to the nuns of Clerkenwell Priory.

The fame of the cure spread, with pilgrimages taking place in August. Indulgences were sold. This was a system that grew up during the Crusades whereby sinners were granted remission of temporal penalties in exchange for payments of money. Undoubtedly the system was abused and was to be attacked by Church reformers. Despite accusations of riotous behaviour by pilgrims, the offerings became a source of income for the priory.

In 1539 the nun's ownership of the Muswell Farm (as it has been called) came to an end when Henry VIII declared himself head of the English Church and seized all Church lands (it was the country's largest landowner at the time). The prioress was required to demise the estate to the King's bottler, John Avery. The estate included a farmhouse, gatehouse, house, storehouse and chapel, presumably all located on the east side of Colney Hatch Lane. During excavation undertaken in the 1930s to facilitate the building of a Roman Catholic church on a site opposite the farm on the west side of Colney Hatch Lane, a headless statue was found and identified as a statue of St Mary, dating from the thirteenth century. This is most likely to have come from the nuns' chapel but cannot be taken as evidence that the chapel stood on this side of the lane. Possibly it had been buried to preserve it.

The nun's priory stood adjacent to St James' church in Clerkenwell and when their land in Muswell Hill was sequestered by the Crown the parish claimed jurisdiction over it. It did this on the grounds that the nuns had not paid tithes to the Rector of Hornsey and was therefore not part of Hornsey parish. Under the tithe system a tenth part of the main crops such as corn, wood etc was paid to the local incumbent. (The system was altered to a rental charge by the 1836 Tithe Commutation Act and abolished a century later). As a result a separate parish authority for part of Muswell Hill came into being, known as Clerkenwell Detached, later marked on the nineteenth century Ordnance Survey map as being 64.542 acres in extent. This, it seems, did not cause problems until housing began to be built on the land in the last quarter of the nineteenth century, when disputes arose between Hornsey and Clerkenwell over such matters as sewage disposal. The land reverted to Hornsey in 1900.

The well on this land survived till the very end of the nineteenth century, providing water for those local inhabitants without access to private wells, which were to be found on private estates. They were to be described by Clerkenwell historian William J Pinks as:

'two in number, and continue in good preservation, being bricked round to the depth from which they seemingly spring (about five feet and a half) and enclosed from the field where they are situated by wooden railings. Though only a few yards asunder, their water differs in quality; that of one being hard, sweet and beautifully pellucid, while the other more nearly resembles rain water and is used only for the purposes for which the latter is applied. Neither is supposed to possess any medicinal properties. By the united and ceaseless overflowing of these wells, a rivulet is formed and named after them the Mose or Moselle, which descending the hill takes a devious course through the parishes of Hornsey and Tottenham…eventually it finds its way into the River Lea at Broadmead Marsh.'

Unfortunately Clerkenwell's suggestion that the wells be preserved as Muswell Hill became urbanized was not taken up, and there is nothing of them to be seen in present day Muswell Road where they were once located.

The Muswell Hill change of ownership, masterminded for Henry VIII by Thomas Cromwell (who was beheaded on Tower Hill in July 1540 after losing the King's support) was part of a great national change. As far as London was concerned, the Crown obtained a substantial amount of land, some of it surviving in the shape of the royal parks and other areas under the control of the Crown Estate Commissioners who still adminster the area around Piccadilly, Pall Mall and Carlton House Terrace. Some, however, was sold to aristocrats such as the Earl of Southampton, who then developed parts of London. All the properties of the Clerkenwell priory were granted away or sold and the last prioress was given an annual pension of £50; she enjoyed this for thirty years, not dying until July 1570. The other nuns also received pensions.

The loss of church lands in London (between 1536 and 1542 all of its thirty or so religious houses were dissolved) occurred when the city began to expand. Its population rose from about 75,000 in 1550 to 200,000 in 1600. It had risen to 400,000 by 1650 and 575,000 by 1700, according to figures quoted by Francis Sheppard in his book *London – A History* (OUP 1998). The sevenfold increase in 150 years was not matched in the rest of England, Sheppard says, where the population did not even double. He argues that the rise in London's population at this time has not yet been adequately explained. During the eighteenth century London became the largest city in the western world.

It would be centuries before the parish of Hornsey and Muswell Hill was seriously affected by London's demographic expansion and topographical extension. Muswell Hill Farm had originated in an undeveloped wooded area. In 1370 over half of the parish of Hornsey was forested with the slow growth of cultivation centred around Crouch End. Much of the manorial lord's demesne wood was reserved for him, and the bishop fenced his park at Highgate and kept his hunting rights until 1660.

Highgate was the most populous settlement in the parish of Hornsey with 161 houses – outside of it the parish had only sixty-two houses. A quarter of the parish was still wooded in 1647, and out of nearly 3,000 acres some 600 were common land. It would be in the seventeenth and eighteenth centuries that woodland clearance gathered pace. It was in this later period that Muswell Hill began to have more estates and more residents.

CHAPTER 2
Distinguished Residents

From the Tudor period onwards, distinguished city figures and even aristocrats were to come to Muswell Hill to take up residence. Several gentlemen and their families held the former nuns' property, including John Avery, William Burnell, William Cowper, Thomas Golding and a London merchant tailor, John Goodwyn, after whom present day Goodwyns Vale was named.

The most important was the Rowe family which was to include three Lord Mayors of London and Sir Thomas Roe, a notable courtier and explorer who had extensive land holdings not only in Muswell Hill, Hornsey, Finchley and Clerkenwell but also in Kent where the family originated. When writing about the holy well John Norden referred to the site of the chapel 'where now Alderman Roe hath fixed a proper house'. This mansion was to be leased in 1601 to Bartholomew Mathewson and is recorded as 'Mattysons' on a map of Tottenham prepared in 1619 by the Earl of Dorset – the house is just across the boundary and is marked as the residence of Sir Julius Caesar. Caesar seems to have been the first courtly resident in Muswell Hill. His father was Adelmare Caesar, a native of Padua who became medical adviser to Queen Mary in 1558 and then to Queen Elizabeth. Julius trained for the law and became an eminent judge as did his brother (Sir) Thomas Caesar. Julius Caesar was to become a Member of Parliament, Chancellor of the Exchequer in 1606 and Master of the Rolls to James I in 1614. He held the post until 1636, when he died aged seventy-nine.

The mansion probably stood on the former farmland close to Colney Hatch Lane and near the wells. Its size can be gauged from the Hearth Tax returns, levied from 1662 to 1689 on large houses, with a tax of ten shillings per hearth. In 1664 Thomas Rowe's mansion contained eighteen hearths. He had it demolished in 1677 but retained the site. Buildings said to be the grange of Rowe's (an outlying grain depository) were blown down in 1707.

The Rowe family were to build other mansions at Muswell Hill. John Warburton's map of Middlesex, first published in 1725, shows two mansions on the north-east side of the hill and one by the road junction with Southwood Lane. The two at the top of the hill came to be known as Bath House and The Grove and the other as The Limes. The first two

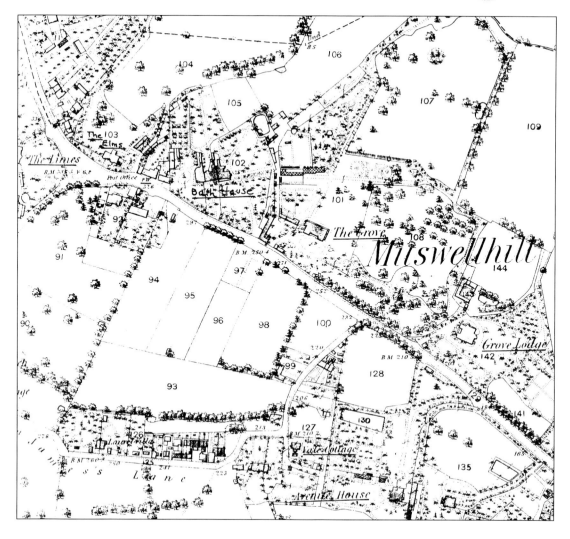

Early estates shown on an 1865 OS map.

survived until 1870 and The Limes until 1896. It would seem that at least two of these mansions, Bath House and The Limes, were Rowe properties, according to the will of Sir Thomas Rowe (1641-1696), which reads:

> 'Whereas Muswell Hill is now double the value of what it once was when my father left it to me and whereas I have bought one house of my sister Mary and built a new house on the common, whereby the copyhold estate is much increased, I do therefore order that my wife enjoy her joynture and that my son Thomas Rowe do have all the rest of the estate being around £220 a year. After decease of my wife I give him the whole estate at Muswell Hill, hoping he will be a good husband and leave this to his [heir] and I with great [deal] of paine and care have preserved it for him.'

The Limes shortly before demolition.

The one built on the common is almost certainly the mansion which came to be called The Limes. Warburton's map does not show a mansion on Muswell Hill Common itself, but waste or common land lay on each side of medieval roads and we can speculate that this was where Rowe built. The land on which he built, at the top of the hill (approximately where the public library is in Queen's Avenue), was flat and a suitable site. Warburton's map shows this as the location of the mansion, and its development with cultivated gardens is to be seen in later maps.

The name Bath House is explained by the fact that the branch of the Rowe family holding land in Muswell Hill petered out in the early eighteenth century. The estates were sold under the will of Henry Guy who had acquired the rights of the co-heirs. Guy was a wealthy Member of Parliament and guardian to William Pulteney, who was to become Earl of Bath. In 1726 the Muswell Hill properties became Pulteney's, leading to one property becoming called Bath House. It was probably not lived in by the Earl for it acquired a reputation as a house of entertainment. A 1776 description of the county of Middlesex reported that 'Roe's noble mansion became the property of the Earl of Bath but was lately converted into a public house'. The last surviving member of the Pulteney family was Henrietta Laura, countess of Bath, judged on her death to be the richest woman in England. Henrietta died childless in 1808 and the Muswell Hill properties passed to William Harry Vane, earl of Darlington and later duke of Cleveland. Vane sold the properties in 1810. Bath House Academy, as it had then become was sold for £1,400 to Thomas Milroy of Lombard Street and the adjacent The Green Man went for £1,000 to James Hawkins, the occupant and

victualler. The Limes estate was sold for £5,500 to a man called Abbott Kent. Thus aristocratic ownership by the Earl of Bath and his family of two seventeenth century mansions built by the Rowe family came to an end.

Bath House, used as an Academy.

Details of these transactions are entered in the Hornsey manorial rolls, for this copyhold land legally remained in the ownership of the lord of the manor, in this case the Bishop of London. The word 'copyhold' derives from manorial tenants showing their evidence of entitlement to land in the form of 'copies' of the relevant entries in the manorial court rolls. Over time 'copyhold' has been converted to common law tenure or freehold.

Another aristocratic resident was to have possession of a property in Muswell Hill during the eighteenth century. This was Topham Beauclerk (1739-80) and the house was The Grove. The origin of this estate, which was just below Bath House on the hill, is not known but Dr Joan Schwitzer has shown in an essay in *Lost Houses of Haringey* (1986) that the property seems to date back to the seventeenth century with the name a reference to the surrounding heavily-wooded landscape; there is a mention of 'Muswell Hill-grove' in the seventeenth century manorial rolls. Topham Beauclerk was to lease it as a country residence, in addition to his town house, from 1769-1779.

The Grove in an early nineteenth-century pen and wash drawing.

Topham Beauclerk was a great-grandson of Charles II by his liaison with Nell Gwynn and was said by some to have a resemblance to the monarch. Beauclerk was given his first name in tribute to Richard Topham MP, a friend of his father from whom, in due course, father and then son inherited estates and income. Topham mixed with fellow aristocrats and gambled but had more serious interests in science and learning. He was an avid book collector and amassed a library of 30,000 volumes. He was a Fellow of the Society of Antiquaries, and also of the Royal Society and the Society of Arts, and his considerable intellect and witty conversation was appreciated by the intelligensia of the day. Early in life, whilst at Oxford, he had become a friend of Dr Samuel Johnson and was a member of his circle.

I find pleasure in the fact that the distinguished literary figure whose Dictionary had been published in 1755 visited Muswell Hill. In a letter to a friend James Boswell wrote that 'Mr Johnson went with me to Beauclerc's villa, Beauclerc having been ill. It is delightful, just at Highgate. He has one of the most numerous and splendid private libraries that I ever saw. Greenhouses, hothouse, observatory, laboratory for chymical experiments – in short everything princely'. Beauclerk was apparently keen on his observatory, for he had an astronomer on the premises, and the height of The Grove, with views over the Lea valley, would have been ideal for the use of a telescope. Due to the renown of the estate visitors had to be restricted through the purchase in advance of a ticket to view, sometimes to the annoyance of people who had just hoped to drop in. Dr Samuel Johnson was perhaps the most noted of the visitors to Muswell Hill and the tree-lined walk through The Grove estate lands (now part of Alexandra Park) is known locally as Dr Johnson's Walk. But other eminent visitors included Horace Walpole, the art patron; Joseph Banks, the botanist who sailed with Captain Cook; and John Wilkes, the radical Member of Parliament for Middlesex.

Dr Johnson's Walk in The Grove.

Topham Beauclerk leased The Grove just after he had married Diana Spencer (1734-1808), daughter of the second Duke of Marlborough, after she had divorced the second Lord Bolingbroke with whom she had had three children in an unhappy marriage. Carola Hicks has told the story of this extraordinary woman's life in *Improper Pursuits – The Scandalous Life of Lady Di Beauclerk* (Macmillan 2001). Diana was a talented artist whose work was commissioned for book illustrations and by Horace Walpole and Josiah Wedgwood. She was a friend of Sir Joshua Reynolds, whose portrait of her may be seen in nearby Kenwood House.

After the aristocratic Beauclerks gave up The Grove in 1779, the property was to be occupied by prosperous business people. These included John Porker, city banker; William Johnstone, stockbroker; and William Block, silk merchant, who was to be the last occupant. In 1863 the property was bought to add to adjacent Tottenham Wood Farm, which had been acquired at the same time for the site of Alexandra Park and Palace; inaugural celebrations were held in the grounds.

Down the hill from The Grove lies another property, the Grove Lodge estate. Part of the grounds survive today, together with a much-renovated mid-nineteenth century house and a lodge house on the side of Muswell

Grove Lodge, which was rebuilt in 1854, shown here in 1960.

Hill. Research by William McBeath Marcham traced the property back to the time of Queen Elizabeth I, when it belonged to Christopher Fulkes, owner of the eastern side of Muswell Hill. After the Civil Wars and Restoration the owner was Sir Paul Paynter (died 1686); the 1664 Hearth Tax records assessed his house as having over twenty hearths. In 1705 Sir George Downing, builder of Downing Street, purchased Grove Lodge from Paynter's widow. In 1708 it was bought by the Dickens family, though the northern part was sold to John Porker, the banker who took over The Grove, leaving the remainder as a separate Grove estate. The subsequent history is detailed by Joyce Horner in an article in Hornsey Historical Society's Bulletin 37 (1996); occupants were to be City attorney William Ashurst, jeweller George Attenborough, who rebuilt the house in 1854 and surveyor John Abraham, who died in 1912 but whose family continued to own the estate till in 1945 Colonel Abraham gave it to the Red Cross which has been using it during the Second World War. The property now belongs to Haringey council which partly rebuilt the 1854 house among other changes. The surviving estate grounds contains some rare trees and is in a conservation area.

The roadside lodge for the Grove Lodge estate once faced a similar building across the road. This was for the Avenue House estate, probably developed in the eighteenth century on former common land. On its twenty-three acres stood not only Avenue House but also Rookfield House and a property called Lalla Rookh, the latter occupied for six months in 1817 by the poet Thomas Moore (1779-1852), after one of whose poems the house was named. Vale Cottage in St James' Lane is a surviving building from the estate. From 1847 Avenue House was owned

Lalla Rookh.

The Elms, with The Green Man on the right.

by Richard Clay, member of an important printing family (the firm still operates, from Bungay, Suffolk). In 1899 the whole estate was purchased by W.J. Collins and developed with housing by him; the Rookfield Garden Estate now occupies the former grounds, with the site of Avenue House now occupied by Nos 19 and 21 Rookfield Avenue.

The Elms stood at the top of the hill, overlooking the road junction, and probably dated from the eighteenth century as well. Covered in ivy in later years it had once faced the village pond, now the site of the roundabout. Its eleven acres were purchased in 1900 by James Edmondson, who laid out Duke's Avenue across it after demolishing the house.

The Hall in Muswell Hill Road is shown on Warburton's map and may have been built before the eighteenth century. The steep part of the road here, now known as Muswell Rise, was once called Brettle's hill after the owner of the house John Brettle, who seems to have extended the estate in the eighteenth century. Still shown on the 1894 OS map, the house was to survive until the end of the nineteenth century. The Hall was the Brettle country residence for they also lived in London's Bedford Row. John Brettle was a lawyer who in 1758 was made secretary to the Stamp Office, which administered a parliamentary tax on legal documents. He was succeeded in the post by his son, also John Brettle, who had married the daughter of Lord Hawley. The second John Brettle, as well as being a Justice of the Peace, was also a volunteer officer with the Middlesex Militia where he rose to be a lieutenant colonel and was known as Colonel Brettle.

There is a tradition that George III visited the Hall, according to the Highgate local historian John Lloyd; the King apparently inspected the

Thomas Moore – a sketch published in 1824.

magnificent cedar tree that then graced the grounds. Lloyd also quotes the memoirs of a Miss Hawkins, which, whilst praising Colonel Brettle's honourable way of dealing, remark upon his parsimony:

'He had a town house which was not only to the last degree dirty, but his villa, on one of the most beautiful eminences north of London, was in a condition that would have deterred many from sleeping in it, even in a moderate breeze. He and his lady, who was of the most grotesque appearance, but of the most lively good humour were at perfect ease with persons of particular distinction, and whose notice conferred honour.'

Thus Brettle was another resident who had access to courtly circles but who enjoyed the rural peace of Muswell Hill. Brettle died in April 1801 and his wife in December 1802. Miss Hawkins wrote:

'He had passed the age of ninety and had been for some time confined to his bed. A violent cough attended his gout, and a spasmodic fit seizing him whilst giving orders to his coachmen for the payment of some bills, he expired with a canvas bag of cash in one hand and a rouleau of banknotes in the other.'

Lloyd recounts a story that a groom took a position at the Hall so that he could pursue his activities as a highwayman from there; this he confessed to Brettle whilst in his death cell at Newgate prison. Lloyd says that 'the position of the old house, surrounded as it then was by the common lands, and in the immediate proximity of Gravel Pit and Coalfall Woods, would render it most desirable as an easy and safe retreat – and who would suspect the trusted groom of a resident householder to be a highwayman?' This area, with Finchley Common to the north, was notorious for this kind of robbery. But crime always exists, and takes many forms. A 1777 newspaper report reads:

'On Monday a man was examined before William Britell, Esq., on a charge of stealing twenty four guineas from out of the house of Mr Huggins, a Farmer, of Muswell Hill; it appeared on examination that the prisoner, in company with another not yet taken, went to the prosecutor's house during Divine Service, on Sunday morning last, under pretence of asking after his health, as he formerly was a lodger in the house, that his accomplice went out under pretence of going to the privy, when he took a ladder and got in at a window on the first floor, from whence he stole the above money; he was committed to New Prison'.

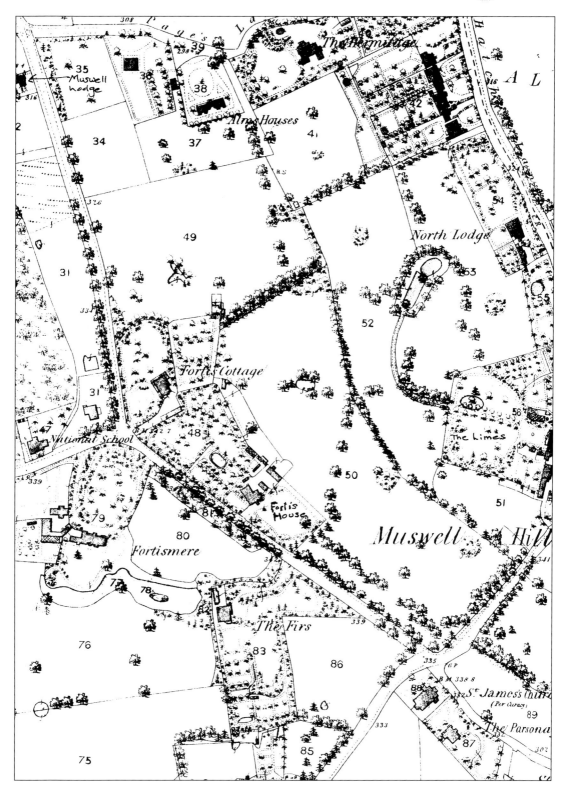

Muswell Hill estates shown on an 1865 OS map, with four villas above North Lodge in Colney Hatch Lane.

North of the Hall stood Fortismere and another house called The Firs. According to Draper these developments were facilitated by the acquisition of parcels of village waste or common from the parish, with John Brettle and Michael Hodgson allowed in 1784 by the parish vestry to have 'part of the common on Fortress Green, Muswell Hill'. According to Draper it was Hodgson who began to build the estate. Shown on the 1816 Hornsey Enclosure Award map, they were to survive until early in the twentieth century when taken by W.J. Collins for building; they are commemorated in the names of two of the avenues he built over their land.

Fortis House stood across the road from Fortismere. A remnant of its mid-nineteenth century coach house survives as No. 38 Princes Avenue and the corner garden was created to save a giant cedar tree which once stood in front of the house. Fortis House was at least eighteenth century in origin. The estate was contiguous to that of The Limes and was at times in the same ownership. It was over the joint estates that, in 1896, Edmondson was to begin to build the modern suburb of Muswell Hill. Known owners in the nineteenth century of Fortis House included George Maynard, the Somes family and James Hall Renton; in 1876 Renton was to extend his property to the north into the east side of Tetherdown when he acquired an eleven-acre estate called Fortis Cottage, (though the house had gone).

Another eighteenth century estate, identified by Dr Draper, was situated in St James's Lane and was known as Kutzleben Hall. The property was named after Baron von Kutzleben, Kutzleben being a small German principality that existed in the days before Germany was united in the nineteenth century. The Baron came to England in 1771, and in 1780 married the daughter of an English baronet. According to Draper, the official name of the mansion was 'My Lord's House in the Bushes' but it was later known as St James's House. The front garden was enclosed from the waste, with parish agreement. In January 1787 Kutzleben was recalled to Hesse-Kassel but did not go, preferring to stay. He died at Muswell Hill on 28 August 1798. St James's House was later divided into three and still stood in 1891.

Thus these country residences for prosperous gentlemen, businessmen and professionals slowly came to dominate the landscape of Muswell Hill. To those already mentioned can be added Belle Vue Lodge, Summerlands, Hillfield, Highfield, Woodside, Wellfield and North Lodge, all still to be seen on the 1894 Ordnance Survey map, along with the Colney Hatch Lane villas and the St James's Lane village cottages, in a still undeveloped area. These small estates usually had some ornamental gardens, avenues of trees, and pasture on which horses and cattle grazed with meadows used for haymaking. Mature trees gave an air of seclusion.

Established farms also existed in the area. Opposite the Hall, approximately where Cranley Gardens begins on the east side of Muswell Hill Road, stood Upton Farm. It occupied over forty-two acres, stretching towards Crouch End at Park Road, where a medieval ecclesiastical demesne farm called Rowledge, belonging to the Bishop of London, still existed. Some of it is still preserved as open land today, as Crouch End Playing Fields. After Upton Farm was bought in 1885 by the Imperial Property Investment Company its fields were built over, Collins laying out Church Crescent at its north end near St James's church.

On the north side of Muswell Hill was Coppetts Farm, the farmhouse dating from 1670 (it was to survive until 1933). This dairy farm lay close to the uncleared Coldfall Wood. Nearby, in Colney Hatch Lane was Muswell Farm, though this was in the parish of Friern Barnet. To the south of it was Tottenham Wood Farm, mostly in the parish of Tottenham but partly in Clerkenwell Detached and partly in Hornsey parish. Its name

Coppetts Farm just before demolition in 1933.

Coppetts Road, leading to the farm, in 1890.

Tottenham Wood Farmhouse. Only the portico now remains.

derived from Tottenham Wood, which till the middle of the eighteenth century covered the hill on which Alexandra Palace stands, located at the western end of Tottenham. Auctioned off by the lord of the manor of Tottenham in 1789 it was bought by a Londoner called Mr Mitchell who built a new farmhouse. Subsequently it belonged to Thomas Rhodes, and following his death in 1856 at the age of ninety-three it was bought as a site for the development of Alexandra Park and Palace.

Although some arable farming existed, most local land was used for meadow or pasture. Rhodes for example aimed to stock his farm with a thousand cows. Haymaking tended to be important, its product being used to feed the population of horses used for transport in London. Market gardening tended to be in other parts of Middlesex.

Not only Muswell Hill but also Crouch End and other parts of Hornsey parish tended to be dominated by small estates owned by prosperous Londoners. The parish vestry became the centre of local government. Its nucleus was in the church minister, churchwardens, overseers of the poor, and highway surveyors who coalesced from the early sixteenth century to form vestries responsible for church fabric, roads, the poor, and finance. In 1601 the Poor Law Act had introduced 'poor rates', local taxes specifically for expenditure on the poor. These were followed in 1654 by highway rates, with parish rate-payers having the right to attend vestry meetings. Both ecclesiastical and civil functions were dealt with, a practice that was to continue throughout the nineteenth century. The manor courts declined in importance.

In the minutes of Hornsey vestry can be found the problems that had to be dealt with. Up to the mid-nineteenth century the vestry controlled a rural parish that had only about 230 houses in 1700 and no more than about 700 in 1800. Highgate was the most populous part and business was divided between Hornsey Side and Highgate Side, with two churchwardens, two overseers of the poor, two highway surveyors and two constables. A paid vestry clerk organised vestry meetings and kept the minutes. From 1774 there was a beadle (who received a new hat and coat every three years) who supervised the workhouse poor and kept order in church and in the village on Sundays. The churchwardens, highway surveyors, overseers and constables were unpaid local people who often sought to avoid being appointed, especially as it might mean their being out of pocket.

Hornsey vestry meetings were usually held on Sundays, either at the church or at a local public house such as the Three Compasses. In the eighteenth century these meetings do not appear to have been attended by the rector. Apart from the officers only about eleven local residents attended on average, even though there were at least 220 households. Those who attended would most likely have been the local gentry rather than the agricultural and other workers who made up the majority of inhabitants.

Most of the parish business was concerned with the poor, the assessment of individual rate liability and its collection, the 1601 Poor Law having given vestries the authority to levy this tax. By 1743 the parish had a workhouse in Hornsey High Street administered by a master and a mistress; the young were apprenticed out to tradesmen and craftsmen.

For the administration of the law there existed, apart from parish vestries, Justices of the Peace. Begun in medieval times as a royal appointment, in later centuries they provided valuable unpaid service. They had jurisdiction over many indictable offences and responsibility for licensing of alehouses and for the appointment of some of the parish officers such as the overseers of the poor and the constables. The post of JP still continues, albeit with different functions, to this day.

Hornsey people were represented in parliament by two elected representatives for the county of Middlesex, voted for by freeholders. Parliamentary representation had begun in 1282 when Knights of the Shire represented the counties; Middlesex representatives had included Sir Roger Cholmely, founder of Highgate school who sat in 1554, and Francis Bacon in 1592. Hornsey was to have separate representation as a constituency in 1885.

Londoners living in Middlesex in the eighteenth century were often opposed to the government and perhaps the greatest expression of their rebelliousness was the election of John Wilkes as MP for Middlesex in

1768. Prosecuted by the government, and outlawed for libel, he was expelled from the House of Commons in 1768 but returned, unopposed, by Middlesex electors in an election subsequently declared void. This was followed by another election in which he was again voted in by the electorate, 'Wilkes and Liberty' having become a popular call. In 1771 Wilkes was elected sheriff of London and Middlesex, and was Lord Mayor of London in 1774, the year he entered Parliament, having again been returned for Middlesex unopposed.

What part, if any, Muswell Hill residents played in this political battle cannot be easily ascertained. We do know, however, that John Wilkes was a visitor to The Grove during Topham Beauclerk's tenancy. Wilkes died in 1797, one of his achievements being to obtain the press's right to publish parliamentary reports, Wilkes having used his position as a city magistrate to protect reporters.

CHAPTER 3

A Nineteenth-Century Arcadia

The rural emptiness of Muswell Hill was to continue throughout most of the nineteenth century, even though the rest of the parish of Hornsey was to be urbanized from the 1860s onwards as London expanded. It was to retain its hilltop exclusion until 1896, despite periodic attempts to sell local estates for building.

Land ownership changed after the passing of the 1813 Hornsey Enclosure Act, which led to the disappearance of Hornsey's commons, including Muswell Hill Common, under the subsequent 1816 Hornsey Enclosure Award. This parliamentary act was but one of the 4,000 or so private acts passed between 1760 and 1844 allowing the enclosure of areas of common land; some six million acres in the country were affected. The intention was to make more waste and common land available for agriculture to match the needs of the rising population, an element of the economic change known as the Industrial Revolution. It was considered that local private owners would be able to make good use of the land if it was allocated to them.

The losers were the cottagers who could not longer use the commons for grazing and other activities that helped make them more self-sufficient. In urban areas such as London the loss of common land also deprived poor people of open spaces and was to lead to demands for the provision of public parks. For in the event it was often not agriculture but housing that took the place of wastes and commons; there were a number of villas built on the new fields. Fortunately for Muswell Hill not much building was to follow and the hamlet remained open, distinguished by mature trees and fine views, though more individual houses were built as the century proceeded.

The 1816 Enclosure Award was made by commissioners appointed under the 1813 act. Most land was allocated to existing landowners such as the Bishop of London and the Prebendary of Brownswood, as well as to the Rector of Hornsey, copyholders and the poor, who were given small allotments of land. Some acreage was sold to defray the cost of the exercise. The Award was accompanied by a large map of the whole parish, including Muswell Hill. It shows how little building had then taken place in the area.

Descriptions of Muswell Hill at this time refer to it as a beautiful place. J. Norris Brewer, for example, writing in his book *The Beauties of England and Wales*, published in 1816 says:

'From this elevation are commanded beautiful and varied prospects, and to the credit of modern taste, there are here constructed numerous detached villas, in every respect calculated to embellish a spot so rich in natural circumstances. These are in general of modest, though spacious, proportions and are provided with ample grounds.'

In his description of Hornsey Brewer says that it comprises almost 2,200 acres, a great proportion of which is used for farming purposes, as meadow and pasture land: 'Few villages in the neighbourhood of London still retain so rural a character.'

A year later J. Hassell published his *Picturesque Rides and Walks – 30 miles round the British Metropolis*, and again praise is given:

'Leaving the delightful scenery around Southgate we rise a considerable hill, and at the distance of two miles reach Muswell Hill. Here again is another little paradise; the succession of enchanting scenery with the abundance of noble timber and immense chains of rising hills, all clothed with the richest verdue and encircled with a redundance of wood will captivate and delight the admirers of landscape scenery on this hill.'

Or, to get the flavour of life in this place, one can turn to Frederic Harrison's *Autobiographic Memoirs*, the two thick red-bound volumes of which, dated 1911, I am happy to have on my shelves. Born in 1831, Harrison was to become an eminent philosopher before his death in 1923. In his book he wrote:

'The first years of my life, as I say, were passed in the delicious quiet of a country village, in a really lovely country, in the easy gliding life of a well-to-do family of many children. Our two daily walks; the great North Road at Highgate which to us was a sort of gateway to the big and distant world; the donkey I used to ride; the daily excitement of the four-horse coach into town; the chats with the neighbouring nurses, children and villagers; the little gardens of our own we each laid out with trees, terraces and artificial lakes which would never hold the water we poured in; the linnet, the rabbit, the butterfly catching and the wild flower gathering… these filled up the even tenor of my childish years.

…My childhood was passed be it remembered in the later years of William IV, and the first years of the Queen [Victoria], an age when railways and telegraphs, penny post and steam-boats were in the stage of project and attempt. …We lived in a pretty cottage, on the crest of Muswell Hill, just opposite the big pond which stood in the square at the three cross-ways. The spot, now a mere suburb of the great City, in the thirties was a beautiful and peaceful village, knowing none but rustic sights and sounds, and keeping the ways and notions of the countryside. My memory as a child is fragrant with the quiet sleepy strolls of babies and nurses, innocent happily of perambulators and modern toys, through flowery meadows and shady copses. How well I remember the limpid stillness of the Muswell, and the knolls where the cowslip and violet grew under the oaks on the region now covered by the Alexandra Palace and its grounds. We would wander there all day and meet no one but a carter or a milkmaid. Hornsey village and Highgate were the utmost limit of our excursions, and our principle experience of town life.

'It seems to me but yesterday that I stood gazing intently on the pellucid spring of the Muswell – wondering whence its waters rose…On our Muswell Hill we knew the story and the ailments of every villager; and I well recall the Quaker family of a small baker opposite, and how their wisdom was called in for remedies and suggestions when one of my brothers scalded his chest with a mug of hot gruel and when another was thought to have swallowed a copper penny. There was no doctor within easy call, and the village community was its own apothecary and nurse. A few inhabitants

Pinner Lodge, a surviving villa in Colney Hatch Lane.

who like my father had a daily business in the city went and came in the four-horse coach, the departure and arrival of which was the stirring incident in the life of the Muswell village...Finchley, Hornsey, Highgate, Holloway were rustic villages when I first knew them; and continuous streets ceased, almost everywhere at two or three miles from St Paul's Churchyard. I remember the site of Paddington Station as a market garden.'

The Enclosure Map of 1816 shows the great absence of buildings in Muswell Hill at that time. On the side of the hill, identifiable by their position, are Grove Lodge, The Grove, Bath House, The Green Man and The Elms, with some other smaller buildings marked near them next to the road junction and the pond, and along the east side of Colney Hatch Lane. On the west side of Colney Hatch Lane, near the junction, stands The Limes and opposite it, on the other side of the Highgate road, is another building – possibly Belle Vue, the house where Harrison grew up. Also identifiable are the Hall, Fortis House, The Firs, Fortismere and Fortis Cottage, but there is little else except the cottages in St James's Lane and the Avenue House, Rookfield and Lallah Rookh properties.

Not many more buildings had been erected some fifty years later when the 1865 Ordnance Survey map was published (see pages 21 and 29). In Colney Hatch Lane there are buildings called Wellfield on the east side, while on the other side is North Lodge, a house built in the grounds of The Limes. North of it, roadside villas have been built, three of which survive

Croquet, played on the lawn of Pinner Lodge.

Westfield Lodge, another Colney Hatch Lane villa, although this one is now gone.

The Hermitage, Pages Lane, in 1820.

today in Colney Hatch Lane. In Pages Lane a building shown on the Enclosure map is named as The Hermitage; it stands on the estate known as North Bank where the present day Victorian house probably replaced it. West of this building, in Pages Lane, stand the Almshouses provided in 1861 by a Madame Uzcelli for five poor persons. Next to these is Springfield House. This property was bought in 1907 for a convent, and extended to provide room for a school; it survives today, having been converted into apartments. Also on the map, in Tetherdown, almost opposite Pages Lane, stands Muswell Lodge; this villa was in 1896 the site of the famous Muswell Hill murder. Soon afterwards it was replaced by housing.

A more significant addition to the landscape is St James's church, with the parsonage to the rear. The building of this church had been promoted

The first St James's church.

The Priory, near the foot of Muswell Hill.

by Richard Harvey, Rector of Hornsey from 1829 to 1881, to meet the needs of Muswell Hill's expanding population and to save local people having to travel to either St Mary's parish church in Hornsey village or to the chapel at Highgate in order to worship. The site was donated by local landowner Henry Warner who lived at The Priory, the estate at the foot of Muswell Hill. The new church was designed by the architect Samuel Angell and became a notable feature at the junction of St James's Lane with the Highgate and Fortis Green Roads, distinguished by a tower with a clock and a wooden spire, and later covered with a mantle of ivy. Consecrated in 1842, it was then extended in 1874. Structural problems

St. James's school in its final years.

towards the end of the nineteenth century combined with urbanization of Muswell Hill led to it being demolished and replaced by the church of St James which stands today; the original clock was mounted onto the new church, and remains one of Muswell Hill's oldest features.

With the building of the church Muswell Hill was no longer classified as a hamlet but as a village. As well as a church it also gained a Church school. In the nineteenth century, before the advent of state education, schools were provided by the Churches, aided from the 1830s onwards by government funding. The Church of England built 'National' schools and the nonconformists provided 'British' schools. On a site in Fortis Green (now occupied by Spring House, near Tetherdown) a National school was built. This was designed by the architect Anthony Salvin, who lived locally and was also responsible for designing the National School for East End Road, East Finchley, and his own and his brother's houses in Fortis Green, although he was more usually employed building or rebuilding country houses. St James's School was intended for infants who would go on to attend the National School in Hornsey, but it came to cater for older girls and then older boys. By 1870 the school was taking 100 of Muswell Hill's 164 children aged between five and thirteen, while Hornsey National School took only twenty-one. In later years the building was enlarged, and it survived on the site until 1968 when it moved to a new building in Woodside Avenue.

By 1851 there were 759 people living in 168 separate dwellings north of St James's Lane. An analysis of the 1851 census returns made by Jean Corker for a Middlesex Polytechnic thesis showed that Muswell Hill had by this time a high proportion of professional, merchant and landowning people compared with the neighbouring village of Hornsey. Among the occupations of Muswell Hill residents were those of attorney, bookseller, barrister, gold dealer, customs officer, printer, solicitor, silversmith and jeweller, as well as the merchants, dealers and manufacturers that made up thirty per cent of the population. Some forty-four per cent Jean Corker classes as unskilled labour, including agricultural workers, gardeners, grooms and dairymen – the remainder were skilled, semi-skilled, lower professionals and domestic servants.

Although Muswell Hill with its merchants and professionals had a smaller proportion of agricultural residents than Hornsey village, nevertheless it was still a rural place. The 1865 map shows it ringed with farms, particularly, as previously mentioned, by Upton Farm in the south, Tottenham Wood Farm in the east and Coldfall Farm in the north. In the west was Finchley parish, which had been the subject of an enclosure act in 1811, with its Award published, like Hornsey's in 1816. The boundary between the parishes of Hornsey and Finchley had never been established because most of the lands had been in the possession of the Bishop of London. The two 1816 Awards led to the disappearance of common land in both parishes, with 900 acres of notorious Finchley Common placed in Finchley parish; this land was at first successfully cultivated but in due course, as it degenerated, the land was used for cemeteries and other municipal purposes. Nevertheless farming continued in the area.

Fortis Green village, backing onto Coldfall Wood, in 1865.

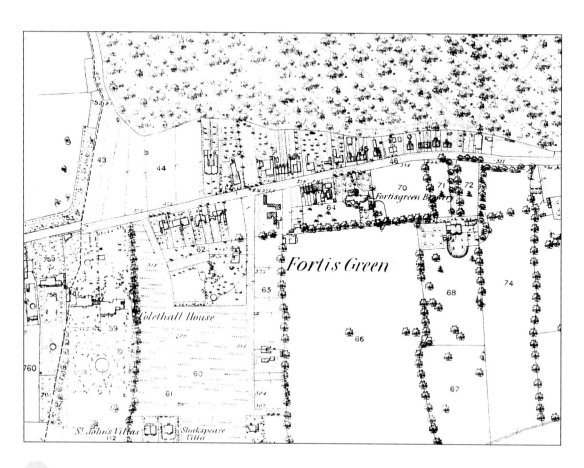

Additionally, the enclosure acts helped lead to the development of Fortis Green, along the road to East Finchley, as a place of residence. Some fine early nineteenth-century houses are still to be seen, particularly at the western end, and two others survive in Southern Road. This became part of the Haswell Park Estate from 1852, comprising Eastern and Western Roads where 180 building plots were laid out, though in the event building up the estate was to take a long time. Along Fortis Green itself weather-boarded cottages were built, some of them now gone, although Field Cottages, Coleraine Cottages and Fortis Green Cottages remind us of the rural village which was developed here in the nineteenth century. Also gone is Fortisgreen Brewery (as it is labelled on the 1865 map), which was replaced in 1904 by the Muswell Hill police station. Still surviving are the Clissold Arms and the Alexandra, once village pubs.

Fortis Green remained a roadside development, with cottages and villas, separated from Muswell Hill until urban development in the late nineteenth century. The building over of the Fortismere Estate by W.J. Collins and the subsequent erection by W.B. Collins of blocks of flats and other properties finally united the two communities to form one urban whole. The clearance of Coldfall Wood aided the process.

What about the people who lived in Muswell Hill estates in the nineteenth century? How did they acquire their wealth and what were their occupations? One of the more interesting estate owners was a Spanish merchant, José (or Joseph) Cayetano de Bernales, a native of Lempias, near Biscay, on the coast of Spain. His London house was 28 Finsbury Place and in his fifties he married a much younger woman called Elizabeth. The fashionable portrait painter of the period was John Northcote RA and evidence exists that in about 1822 Northcote painted portraits of both de Bernales and his young wife, but sadly the location of these, if they still exist, is not known. In 1806, about the time of his marriage to the sixteen-year-old Elizabeth, de Bernales bought The Limes and in 1816 extended his holding to include all the land between Pages Lane, Colney Hatch Lane, the road to Highgate and Fortis Green Road, except for Fortis House and its land, on the east side. He also owned the former bowling green and purchased the northern portion of Muswell Hill Common (sales of land reaped enough income to cover the expenses of the three Commissioners making the awards). Elizabeth died in 1823, aged thirty-two, and in 1824 de Bernales went bankrupt. Sent to the debtors' prison he was discharged in 1825 on the condition that all his property (including, presumably, the portraits) was sold. Within a month de Bernales had died, at the age of seventy-four.

Interestingly, the successive occupants of The Limes during the nineteenth century were each connected in some way with writing, publishing and books. First after de Bernales to reside in the house was William Brodie Gurney, a professional shorthand-writer whose family had

established the Gurney system used extensively in reporting trials – he was to have his name included by Lord Byron in *Don Juan*. Gurney's wife died at Muswell Hill in 1830, causing him to sell up. Next came Richard Marshall (1789-1863) who was a driving force in the book wholesale firm Simpkin and Marshall, a business which was to survive the destruction of its Paternoster Row warehouses during the Blitz and continue trading until the 1960s. Richard Marshall moved into The Limes in 1831 and occupied the estate until 1863, with his daughters marrying locally. Sarah married a member of the Miles family at Highgate with whom Marshall had business connections (a Miles was a partner in the firm of Simpkin and Marshall), and from this marriage two daughters later married into the Clay family that lived at Avenue House on Muswell Hill. Marshall's three daughters were known as the Belles of Muswell Hill; Sarah's sister Emily married a man from Highgate, and the third daughter, Margaret, married Henry John Smith. North Lodge was built as a home for them. More information about Marshall and other occupants of The Limes is given in my chapter in *People and Places – Lost Estates in Highgate*, Hornsey and Wood Green (Hornsey Historical Society 1996).

Whilst Marshall was living at The Limes, Dr Protheroe Smith came to live at The Elms, the Georgian house overlooking the road junction and more or less facing Marshall's residence. Smith was eminent in the medical profession and attended Lord Palmerston, the Prime Minister. Specialising in women's diseases he set up the world's first women's hospital in Red Lion Square, later in Soho Square. He pioneered the use of chloroform in childbirth. Concerned with hygiene he had the Muswell Hill pond outside his house removed in 1858 and replaced by a tank and tap.

Muswell Hill's attraction for professionals from the world of books was underlined when in 1847 Avenue House was purchased by Richard Clay, a printer who, after an apprenticeship in his home town of Cambridge, had successfully set up in the London. The Clays were to be a dynasty of printers whose story can be read in *Clays of Bungay*, by James Moran, published by the firm in 1978. Married at the age of thirty-six to a Cambridge girl called Susanna, the Clays were to have ten children, four of whom died in infancy. One of his sons was to become Cambridge University Printer, and another Richard was to follow him in the business. Three of the Clay children married into local families in Hornsey and Highgate, underlining the social life of the area that brought together young people of similar status.

Outside this circle, but eminent in his own right, was William Tegetmeier who for a period lived in an old weather-boarded house in St James's Lane which still survives. Born in 1816 and alive until 1912, Tegetmeier was of Hanoverian descent and became a naturalist and a journalist and author. His research work on bees, some of it carried out in St James's Lane, is known to have been of value to Charles Darwin in compiling *On the Origin of Species*. Tegetmeier also pioneered pigeon racing, with some pigeon races beginning from Alexandra Palace. In 1868 Tegetmeier moved to a villa called Coldfall Lodge in Fortis Green. His name appears in a diary kept by Marian Chambers, the wife of an architect, who lived in St Martin's villa on Crouch Hill. In 1872 the diary refers to a visit made to Mr Tegetmeier, recording: 'His eyes very bad – dropsy in them.'

Muswell Hill was also home to members of the legal profession. One of renown was William Henry Ashurst (1792-1855), who resided at Grove Lodge. He had radical beliefs and as a solicitor he had refused to pay taxes until the 1832 Reform Bill was passed. He became an under-sheriff of London and helped Rowland Hill, whose family had opened a pioneering school at Bruce Castle, Tottenham, with the development of penny postage, which came into existence in 1840. Movements to unite Italy developed during the nineteenth century and Ashurst was a founder of the Society of Friends of Italy and as such often had as a guest at Muswell Hill the famous Italian patriot Giuseppe Mazzini (1805-72) who had been banished from Italy and who lived in London from 1836 to 1848.

The rural isolation of Muswell Hill in 1846 was recorded by Ashurst's daughter when she edited Mazzini's *Letters to an English Family*:

> 'Muswell Hill, a village on the Hornsey side, was not at that time very accessible. By night no help could be obtained from rail or stage, and cabs being too expensive for most of the habitues, it was customary for the friends who had enjoyed Mr Ashurst's hospitality to assemble in the porch at about half-past ten and journey together on foot as far as the Angel, Islington, where cabs and omnibuses were available.'

Another member of the legal profession was barrister William Manson. By 1860, Bath House, the old mansion on Muswell Hill, was no longer a school but had been divided into three separate dwellings, with Manson living in the centre one. Before his early death, Thomas Rhodes, son of the man who farmed Tottenham Wood Farm, had moved into Wellfield, which was built by William Bird some time after 1826 when he purchased the land. This Wellfield estate had been part of the nuns' farm and had been bought by Rhodes to extend his holdings when William Bird died in 1834. Unfortunately, Thomas Rhodes tried to stop people coming onto Tottenham Wood Farm land to use the old wells which still served as a water supply and Manson was successful in keeping the wells in public use. William Manson's son Frederic moved into Wellfield after the younger Thomas Rhodes died and was also to become the owner of the adjacent property, The Elms. When in 1896 Edmondson came to develop Muswell

Hill as a suburb he was to have vital dealings with Frederic Manson, the biggest local landowner by then.

Other important landowners in Muswell Hill were the Somes family, who possessed Fortismere and whose business was in ship-owning, and on the other side of Fortis Green Road, the stockbroker James Hall Renton (1812-1895), who owned Fortis House and estate, using the latter as a stud farm for horse breeding; his main residence was in London's Park Lane, facing Hyde Park, then a very desirable place to live. These landowners were to play an important role in the history of Muswell Hill. During the period when the Somes family owned The Limes, during the second half of the nineteenth century, they leased it to another prominent figure in the world of books – Charles Edward Mudie, who took up residence in the old mansion in 1867. He was to establish a private circulating library of huge size which, for a fee, loaned books to customers not only in the United Kingdom but as far abroad as China. So after the death of Richard Marshall, the book wholesaler, The Limes was to be occupied by Mudie, the book lender.

A closer involvement with the creative rather than the commercial side of books was to be associated with another Muswell Hill house. This was Woodlands, built around 1850 in Muswell Hill Road on the way to Highgate, and to be occupied from 1861 by the Lehmann family as their country residence. Frederick Lehmann, of German origin was to make his living as a partner in an engineering firm but came from a family with artistic interests. His wife Nina was the daughter of the Scotsman who had edited the first Chambers' Encyclopedia. Woodlands, undoubtedly so

The Woodlands, front view, c. 1890.

named because of its proximity to the woods on each side of Muswell Hill Road, became a place visited by the leading lights of the Victorian cultural world of the 1860s and 70s – details of which are given by Jules Kosky in his chapter in *People and Places – Lost Estates in Highgate, Hornsey and Wood Green*. It is probable that Charles Dickens visited Woodlands and certain that Wilkie Collins did, for he stayed here in 1869 to write the novel *Man and Wife*. The Lehmann descendants were to continue their parents' interest in the arts, their son R.C. Lehmann becoming editor of *Punch*. The grandchildren included the siblings Rosamund Lehmann, the novelist, Beatrice Lehmann the actress and John Lehmann the man of letters who published the periodical *New Writing* in the 1930s and 1940s. Many years ago I read John Lehmann's *Ancestors and Friends* (1962) one of several autobiographical volumes, which recounts the story of Nina and her husband and quotes from a letter by Nina which again emphasises the beauty of the Muswell Hill landscape enjoyed by these local residents:

'If I could only give you a picture that could convey an idea of the brilliant beauty in which Woodlands bathes this morning. The atmosphere is so clear that we see to the Essex hills, over the terraces of trees, the ivy covered tower of Hornsey, the lines of delicious green fields dotted with white houses – sheep – horses – cattle. In the front our own delicious lawn with its graceful Deodars waving slightly in the crisp yet mild morning breeze, the warm sun shining over all – shining into the open window of my little drawing-room where I sit writing to my Beloved, shining on the flowers with which my windows are all alive, shining on my children who are sparkling about the lawn followed fast by their long shadows'.

A literary figure who lived locally, whom the Lehmanns entertained, was the poet Coventry Patmore (1823-96). He resided at Highwood Lodge, between Eastern and Western Roads in Fortis Green. Too late to meet the Lehmanns, who vacated Woodlands in 1875, was W.E. Henley (1849-1903) another poet and literary figure who was to live from 1896 for two years at Stanley Lodge in Tetherdown (now rebuilt). Woodlands had gone by then for it was demolished in 1890 to make way for Woodland Rise housing.

During most of the nineteenth century the village of Muswell Hill revolved around the needs of the occupants of the detached houses and small estates, some of which were primarily owned as summer residences for Londoners. Nevertheless by the 1860s its population numbered about 1000, and by 1891 was just under 2000, and the needs of all of them for food, household goods and services had to be met. The gentry

Coventry Patmore who lived in Fortis Green in the 1860s.

W.E. Henley who lived in Tetherdown 1896-98.

would have sustained themselves to a considerable extent by their own produce garnered from their kitchen gardens and orchards, and from the cows and other animals which grazed on their estates. Local dairy farms were nearby. Horse-drawn carts delivered items from further afield, from shopkeepers in Hornsey and Highgate villages, and from the Holloway establishment of Jones Brothers, where furnishings were sold, and even from West End department stores.

The village itself was poorly served by shops numbering about four. These were around the Green Man and included a post office (so marked on the 1865 map) next to it. This building, which seems from observation to be late eighteenth century, still survives, sandwiched between the rebuilt public house and the Exchange (the shops that Edmondson built in 1900) and must be one of Muswell Hill's earliest surviving buildings. This post office building was by 1890 a general store, and the post office was operated by the Misses Archer from a small shop at the beginning of Colney Hatch Lane on the east side, where there was a cluster of small buildings.

Amongst these was once Boundary House, a property so named because it stood on the boundary line between Hornsey parish and Clerkenwell Detached. Built on this side of the road by 1865 were Castle Villas, which still survive, although their front gardens are taken by single-storey shops. A sketch of them and of Boundary House are to be found in Pinks's *History of Clerkenwell*.

Opposite the old pub there still stands today, jutting out onto the pavement, a building once known as the White House and recently occupied by an estate agent. This is probably also an eighteenth century survivor, and was in use in the middle of the nineteenth century as a butcher's, opening twice a week. Later it became a confectioner's and tobacconist's until occupied by Mr G.H. Smith who carried on a

Boundary House, Colney Hatch Lane, in the early nineteenth century.

large house-decorating business once urbanization occurred. His father Benjamin Smith lived in Pages Lane and employed Charles White, who was to be one of the founders in 1879 of the still-thriving local firm of Bond and White, building supplies merchants. For several decades in the twentieth century the White House was occupied by the estate agency of Alfred Slinn who took it over in 1938.

In 'the old village' of Muswell Hill at the bottom of St James's Lane, settled from at least the eighteenth century, stood less affluent housing where some sixteen properties formed old fashioned alleys. In the lane stood a small weather-boarded public house called The Royal Oak, where local residents were able to buy some articles over the counter, though as I know from personal experience it had an extremely small bar area; room for selling must have been limited. This pub, rebuilt in the 1960s, and the Green Man, were the only two village pubs, but Fortis Green boasted two more already mentioned, plus some five shops.

The visual appearance of Muswell Hill seems to have been dominated by the trees which grew profusely in the area, many of them tall and mature. One of them on the North Bank estate, which was untouched by urbanization is a chestnut said to have begun life in around 1650. The boundaries of the estates seem to have been lined with wooden paling fences and the road surfaces improved only by gravel. Transport

The butcher's shop on Muswell Hill, a nineteenth-century sketch.

49

The Royal Oak, St James's Lane, in 1937.

was by horse-drawn vehicle only. It was a world which was to pass away at the end of the nineteenth century and was lucky to survive so long. It was in the second half of that century that changes foreshadowed what was to happen.

CHAPTER 4
Arcadia under Threat

Muswell Hill was still a small Middlesex village in the second half of the nineteenth century but its proximity to London increasingly meant that it was threatened by the city's expansion. The advent of mechanical forms of transport, developed by the great engineers of the Victorian Age, offered poorly paid workers the opportunity to travel some distance at a fare they could afford and thus live further from their place of work than they previously could. They could begin to live on London's fringes yet travel in to work in its industries and offices.

First came the invention of the steam locomotive and the subsequent building of a vast railway network, and the accompanying realization that short-distance commuter traffic yielded profits as well as long-distance traffic. Then came the horse bus and the horse tram, but more importantly their successors, the petrol bus and the electric tram. Also, of course, a new practical standard bicycle used by both men and women. As transport systems were put into place (including from 1863 the world's first underground railway, which connected London's termini with work destinations) and the city's population expanded, so the hinterland of London was seen as a place to build houses, a profitable investment not only for builders and entrepreneurs but also for landowners, as it yielded them greater returns than agriculture did. Small private estates could be traded in for money. Suburbs that had previously been places dominated by the upper and middle classes could now be a place of residence for people lower down the social scale. As cities grew nastier with manufacturing fumes, stench, crowds, noise and lack of adequate sanitation, a residence away from the city centre became widely sought.

The process was continuous. Prime step was the availability of land, without which no suburb could be developed. But there was usually someone prepared to sell up, or sites up for auction and sale, and so London grew outwards, often along roads and near railway stations as land became available. It was an age when the dominant building form was the terrace, comprised either of comfortably large houses, sometimes three storeys tall, or of meaner two up, two down properties. So the great nineteenth-century web of terraced streets emerged in London, swathes of Victorian housing occupying previous open spaces. In the centre of the city land use intensified. The merchant's counting house used for residence and trading gave way to new purpose-built office blocks, a development emerging in the 1830s.

The parish of Hornsey was affected by the 1860s. In the south the Brownswood estate was developed next to Seven Sisters Road and in the 1870s much of Stroud Green was built up. From the late 1860s rather poor-quality terraced housing began to be built each side of Hornsey High Street at its western end. By 1880 much of Crouch End had begun to be transformed from a small crossroads settlement surrounded by private estates into an urban centre. Among the areas left untouched were the Priory estate, from Middle Lane to the foot of Muswell Hill, and Muswell Hill itself.

The railway had been one engine of change. This had begun in 1850 when Hornsey was the first station outside London on the new main line to the north, built by the Great Northern Railway Company. The terminus opened at Kings Cross in 1852. Soon other lines followed so that between 1850 and 1885, when Harringay West station opened, some ten railway stations were opened up in the area, responding to swift change as the rural parish was urbanized. By 1891 Hornsey's population had reached 61,097 compared with the 19,357 it had been twenty years earlier in 1871. It was to grow still further, reaching 72,056 in 1901. Town had replaced countryside.

Control of local affairs necessarily had to change as the population expanded and a rural environment gave way to a built-up environment. In place of the vestry came Hornsey Board of Health, set up in 1867 under an 1858 Local Government Act after some dilatoriness and resistance to change by Hornsey parish notables. The monogram HLB, for Hornsey Local Board, began to be seen on street furniture. Examples can still be found, including a hydrant cover in the centre of Muswell Hill roundabout. Two years previously an independent board had been set up for South Hornsey, and the area south of Seven Sisters Road became separate from Hornsey proper; in 1899 it was to be included in Stoke Newington local authority.

Hornsey Local Board, headed by H. Reader Williams, liberal, wine merchant and charity worker, set up committees to deal with sewers, water, nuisance removal, finance, roads and works, its fifteen members meeting fortnightly. By 1891 it had the services of a clerk, accountant, solicitor, engineer and surveyor, medical officer of health, rate collectors, sanitary inspectors, building inspectors and road foremen. Their offices were built in 1869 in Southwood Lane, Highgate, and continued to be used until Hornsey Town Hall was built in Crouch End Broadway in 1933-35.

Hornsey Urban District Council replaced Hornsey Local Board in 1894, under parliamentary legislation dealing with local government and

Hornsey Local Board (HLB) fire hydrant cover from 1887.

HUDC began to appear on street furniture instead of HLB. H. Reader Williams retired when the board was replaced and in recognition of his hard work, including saving open spaces, the clock tower in Crouch End Broadway was erected, by public subscription, in his honour with a portrait medallion on it. It was unveiled in 1895, two years before he died. In 1891 only one HLB member lived at Muswell Hill. This was Edward Upton who resided at The Chestnuts, one of several villas between Woodside Avenue and Fortis Green Road on Muswell Hill Road. Hornsey UDC was to exist only until 1903 when Hornsey successfully achieved borough status in recognition of its size and the monogram BH began to appear on hydrant covers and the like. Muswell Hill began to be governed by borough councillors.

Hornsey Urban District Council (HUDC) hydrant cover set in the pavement in Muswell Hill.

In 1885 Hornsey became one of seven Middlesex Divisions returning Members to Parliament, where before there had been just two representatives for all Middlesex – the whole area was by now being widely urbanized. In 1891 the MP was Henry Stephens of the Stephens Ink firm who lived at Church End, Finchley. The constituency at that time included Finchley, Hornsey, South Hornsey and some outvoters. In 1918 Hornsey became a Parliamentary borough. It returned Unionist or Conservative members until 1992 when Labour MP Barbara Roche was elected. Mrs Roche, a lawyer, became a junior member in the Blair government and moved into a house in Muswell Hill.

Muswell Hill, in the north of the parish and the furthest away from London, remained untouched, but attempts to develop its estates for housing were nevertheless made. The first was in 1863 when Richard Marshall of The Limes died. The estate was bought by the London and County Building Company and then put up for auction in lots. One local landowner realized the impact of such development on his rural arcadia and bought the whole estate. This was the Somes family, living at Fortismere. Soon afterwards they leased The Limes estate to C.E. Mudie, like themselves a businessman who wanted a place in the country. Mudie moved into The Limes mansion with his two sons, five daughters and his indoor and outdoor servants where he was to continue to live until 1887. By then of course, saddened by the death at age twenty-nine of the son who was helping him to run the business, and in poor health himself, he would have forseen that the arcadia was coming to an end. A comment in a trade paper of 1885 pointed it out. After saying that Charles Mudie, the founder of the circulating library was a sociable man it said that he was 'in the habit of giving high entertainments at his garden parties in the comfortable house on the top of Muswell Hill', and went on, 'the Muswell house is still a fine country residence, though there is now a railway station near, and the bricks and mortar are filling the vacant green slopes which have been so dear to many generations of Londoners'.

In 1880 there was a second threat to the Muswell Hill arcadia when the Georgian mansion The Elms, at the top of Muswell Hill overlooking the road junction, was put up for sale. It was advertised as 'Being also highly valuable for development as a Building Estate'. Its accompanying sale map outlined a 'suggested new road' across its eleven acres. Fortunately this did not happen and it would be another twenty years before the suggested new road materialized in the form of Dukes Avenue, built by Edmondson.

The third attempt was made five years later when Avenue House, along with twenty-three acres on the side of Muswell Hill containing various other properties, was put on the market. It was described as being 'well adapted for the erection of superior residences and for residences of a smaller character'. It was not sold and it came on the market again at the end of the century when it was bought by the builder W.J. Collins in 1899. Soon afterwards Collins built houses on the perimeter of the estate, and also laid out Etheldene Avenue. He then planned the development of the rest of the grounds, a project that was later taken over by two of his sons. It resulted in the Rookfield Garden estate.

The first suburban roads were laid out in the late 1880s. These included Muswell Road and Muswell Avenue and other roads on the northern side of Clerkenwell Detached. This followed the sale of a portion of land by the London Financial Association – which by then owned the Alexandra Park Estate – in a desperate effort to improve their financial situation. The story of this venture now needs to be told.

It begins in the early part of the nineteenth century when Thomas Rhodes acquired Tottenham Wood Farm, went into dairy farming and extended his land holdings till they reached 470 acres. He died in 1856 at the age of ninety-three, having outlived his son. By then his farmland stretched east from Colney Hatch Lane as far as the 1850 Great Northern Railway line. Located as it was on the edge of Muswell Hill village, its fate was bound to affect local people. Events showed that Thomas Rhodes's family did not seem to want to continue farming. The estate was put up for auction on 4 August 1858, the sale notice indicating that the 470 acres included the farmhouse itself (its portico survives in Rhodes Avenue) with its lawns, kitchen gardens, 'melon grounds', carriage yard and Baliff's cottage, meadow and park-like land, the latter being described as 'beautifully undulating' and 'possessing charming views'. These had been divided into plots of various sizes 'admirably adapted for the erection of first class villas'. 'The Great Northern Railway,' it was written, 'passes through a cutting on the Wood Green side of the Estate where a Station is to be made.'

The station was indeed built and opened in 1859 as Wood Green station (now known as Alexandra Palace). According to testimony by the general manager of the railway at an 1864 enquiry into further railway proposals, the sum of £4,000 had been paid towards the cost of this new station by Mr Rhodes, the owner of the adjacent estate. 'They wanted to make it into a residential place,' the railway manager said, 'and they subscribed the money in order to enhance the value of the land to make a station.'

It could have been that these grandiose plans to use the farm for villas were devised by the Rhodes family. But significantly the plan that accompanies the auction prospectus and which is marked out with the plot details has one plot marked as 'reserved'. This is the one at the top of the hill where eventually Alexandra Palace was to be built. This links it with the project to build a giant glass exhibition building in north London that would rival the one recently erected (1854) in south London at Sydenham. Designed by Paxton, the south London building had been originally erected in Hyde Park to house the 1851 International Exhibition and had been dubbed by *Punch* magazine the 'Crystal Palace', a name it would retain until it was burnt down in 1936.

In my short history of Alexandra Palace and Park entitled *Palace on the Hill* (Hornsey Historical Society, 2nd edition 1994) I detail the role of the architect Owen Jones (1809-76) in this venture. Closely involved with Paxton in the Crystal Palace, Jones went on to exhibit drawings in December 1858 for a similar Crystal Palace at Muswell Hill. An accompanying pamphlet describes the advantage of the site, which by then he had obviously found in the vacant Tottenham Wood Farm. He refers to the site's 'elevated position' with 'extensive and beautiful views' and its proximity to a great trunk railway. Jones's pamphlet describes the proposed building and sets out the underlying reasons for it:

'In designing the building the Architect has endeavoured to combine the objects which the Promoters have in view viz "to afford on a large scale the means of Intellectual Improvement and Physical Recreation to the masses, with such features of Design as should render the Building itself attractive, a point of great importance to a Self-Supporting Institution."'

The pamphlet explains that in one of two naves of the building, 'there may be a permanent Exhibition of the Works of Industry and the Objects of Commerce' while 'in the other, the Arts and Sciences which direct and embellish the Products of Industry may find their appropriate home'.

Jones's proposals were very much the essence of the Victorian age. The Industrial Revolution had seen a change from individual craft manufacture in domestic locations to factory-based industry, with mass production the key to the financial success of the entrepreneurs. It was realized over a period of time that design was still important and needed

The burning of the first Alexandra Palace in June 1873.

to be promoted, that workers needed to be informed and educated about their work and that, for the benefits of mass production to be fully realized, the product had to be marketed and brought to the attention of potential customers at home and abroad. These motivations had an important consequence – the development of public exhibitions of products, at which their design and technical development could be demonstrated. Both England and France began to move in this direction in the late eighteenth century, in England with the Society of Arts and later the development of Workmen's Institutes.

The French originally had intended to stage the world's first international exhibition, with stands from foreign countries, but when they failed to do so Britain gained this honour with the 1851 exhibition in Hyde Park. The concept spread rapidly through Europe and North America, and the erection of exhibition buildings with displays that combine education and entertainment persists to this day. Alexandra Palace, conceived in 1858 was an early example, finally opening its doors in 1873.

West view of the burning palace.

Although the hilltop site was inaugurated in 1859 the great glass building designed by Jones was never built because the promoters could not finance it. Nevertheless another company pursued the idea and purchased the farm in 1863. They added to it the then-vacant Grove estate so that there could be pedestrian access to the hill from the village of Muswell Hill. This resulted in the creation of Alexandra Park, named after the young Danish princess who that year had married the future Edward VII. Work then began on the creation of a park area of some 200 acres in the southern part of the farm, the creation in it of a racecourse, and the building of the People's Palace, to be served by a branch railway from Highgate. The rest of the farmlands to the north of the park were left untouched and the villas proposed originally (perhaps similar to those built in Regents Park or which lined Victoria Park, or were later proposed for Finsbury Park) were never to materialize. Building of the first Alexandra Palace was completed by 1866 but was not opened until the railway was completed in 1873. It was burnt down soon after opening and replaced by the second Alexandra Palace, opened in 1875, the main fabric of which remains.

The significance for Muswell Hill was that four hundred acres on its eastern side remained undeveloped until a small acreage adjacent to Colney Hatch Lane was sold in the 1880s. As demand for building land increased in the last decades of the nineteenth century it was seen that the Alexandra Palace estate, both park and undeveloped land, might be covered with housing. Local authority councillors therefore purchased in 1900 the park and palace to save the open space. The northern part of the park was not preserved and it gave way to The Avenue and surrounding roads, while the northern part of the estate was also used for housing, with houses in locations such as Owtram and Princess Avenue date-stoned

The burning of Central Transept.

The rescuing of art treasures from the burning palace.

Getting out the last of the art treasures.

1901. Fortunately a large part of this northern part of the estate had been acquired in 1893 for Muswell Hill Golf course, and some of the other land was used by Wood Green council for schools, a lido and the Albert Road recreation ground. So between Friern Barnet Town Hall and the hill much of the land is still open space – the grounds of former Friern Hospital, opened as Middlesex County Lunatic Asylum in 1851, still form a northern extension of this space, despite being used for other purposes.

Preservation of the ancient woodland between Muswell Hill and Highgate also played an important part in preventing Muswell Hill from being densely built up. Campaigning led to the acquisition of Highgate Wood by the Corporation of London in 1886, and of the former Churchyard Bottom Wood opposite it by Hornsey council in 1894. The latter was renamed Queens Wood in honour of Queen Victoria. These two areas of woodland, straddling Muswell Hill Road, form a green barrier to the south. Both areas could have been sold off for housing.

The second Alexandra Palace of 1875, south front.

The Grand Hall, with organ, at Alexandra Palace.

Arrival of the Prince of Wales at Alexandra Palace, 1876, with the Four-in-Hand Club.

Pigeon racing at Alexandra Palace; at the rear is a now lost circus building.

Whilst The Limes, The Elms, Avenue House and Tottenham Wood Farm all escaped being built over in the second half of the nineteenth century, there was still a steady addition to the number of houses in the village. The south side of what is now Muswell Hill Broadway was lined with Belle Vue, Summerlands, The Villa, Hillfield Cottages, Stanley Villa, Rosemount and then a late Victorian house called Hillfield, which was occupied in the 1890s by a scientist named William Barlow. Down Muswell Hill Road, towards Highgate, were built Norton Lees (erected 1875), Roseneath and Lea Wood, in what was to become Woodside Avenue. These three Victorian houses are now incorporated into St Luke's Hospital.

*Looking west towards
Alexandra Palace, 1884.*

Opposite St James's church a terrace of substantial houses with long gardens (now the site of the Odeon complex) was built around the 1880s. In Tetherdown a substantial mansion called Woodside, built before 1865, stood on the corner with Fortis Green, backing onto Coldfall Wood. Tetherdown itself began to acquire houses, including villas called Newport, Blymhill and Thornton, but also smaller terraces (a date stone for 1873 can be seen). These were on the west side. Half of the eastern side was Renton's undeveloped land but north of this three tall pairs of Victorian houses with Gothic gables were put up (now Nos 58-60) along with other properties, including glass houses. On the Pages Lane corner with Coppetts Road into which Tetherdown runs (in 1891 the whole road was still known as Tatterdown Lane) was built a group of cottages

*Queen's Wood, with
Keeper's Lodge.*

and small houses known as Tatterdown Place, probably dating from around 1870. Opposite them in Pages Lane stand Myrtle Villas, adjacent to Springfield House. One of these two houses was used as 'Mrs Hart's Home for Little Girls'; this local charity, dating from the 1880s, housed about a dozen children whose mothers had died or had been forced to abandon them. It was founded by Mrs Percival Hart of Highgate.

The lack of any substantial development disproves the theory that the arrival of a railway station will always lead to residential building. For since 1873 Muswell Hill had had its own railway station, built on the branch line to Alexandra Palace and thus providing easy access to Kings Cross and the City. Some development followed the opening of the station, with the building nearby of Grosvenor Gardens, which are a group of substantial properties, and with the laying out opposite of Muswell Hill Place and Alexandra Place (later called Alexandra Gardens). But by 1894 only five houses had been built on these last two roads, though a Village Club had been erected, promoted by St James's church to cater for the social needs of those in the old cottages in St James's Lane.

The lack of desire by the occupiers of the estates to surrender their arcadia for money must have been one factor in the late development of Muswell Hill. Another was its hilly nature, which could deter builders who found the flatter lands of Hornsey more accessible as well as being nearer to London. It was when James Hall Renton died in 1895 and the combined grounds of Fortis House and The Limes, between Fortis Green Road and Colney Hatch Lane, came onto the market that a developer seized the opportunity to build a new suburb. Again, one factor was the flat nature of these thirty acres. So in 1896, when James Edmondson purchased the estate, the Muswell Hill arcadia of green trees and lawns, of dazzling views and a rural economy was to end. The Muswell Hill that we know today was about to come into being.

CHAPTER 5

Houses on the Hilltop

As if symbolic of coming change, an elderly resident in one of Muswell Hill's detached houses was murdered on 14 February 1896. The scene was Muswell Lodge, Tetherdown, which stood opposite Pages Lane; there seventy-eight-year-old Henry Smith resided, in a detached house backing onto Coldfall Wood. Fearing intruders, he had run a trip wire across his garden that would fire a gun as a warning. This proved no obstacle to two criminals, Albert Milsom and Henry Fowler – the latter a man of violence on parole from prison – who forced their way in through a window one night and murdered Smith when he disturbed them. An abandoned oil lantern linked the robbery to Milsom and soon Milsom and Fowler were being trailed across the country in their attempt to keep out of sight. Arrested in Bath on 10 April 1896, they were convicted at the Old Bailey on 19 May and hanged, side by side, on 10 June, four months after the murder.

On Sunday 16 February, just after the murder, some 15,000 to 20,000 people came to see the scene of the crime, according to the local paper, the *Hornsey Journal*. Later that year, when Muswell Hill began to be built up, it was claimed that the publicity brought about by the murder

Muswell Lodge, 1882.

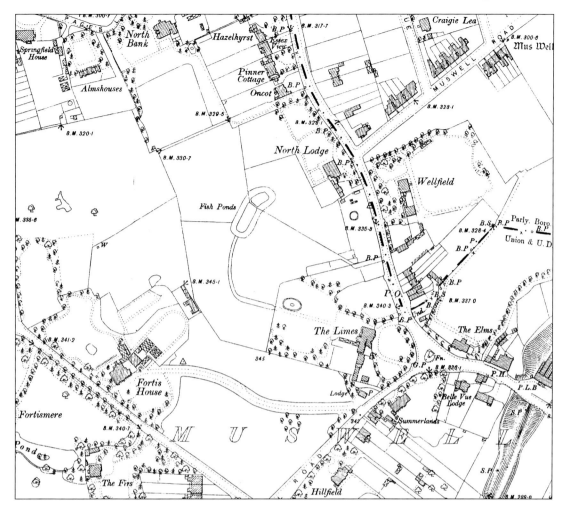

had attracted attention to the area, which had contributed to its being developed. This was not true.

Newspaper proprietor William Cummins reminisced in his local paper, the *Muswell Hill Record* that James Edmondson, the man who was to create the new suburb, had come across Muswell Hill 'whilst out for a spin on his cycle', and saw its advantages as a prospective suburb. It is to Edmondson and not to the publicity following a murder that we owe the development of Muswell Hill. But even so, it would not have been possible without the availability of land on which to build, and by chance Edmondson managed to secure the jointly owned Fortis House and The Limes estates.

James Hall Renton, who had owned this land between Fortis Green Road and Colney Hatch Lane, which also stretched up into Tetherdown, died in January 1895. Legal documents show that the estate was first sold to a local landowner in the same year, but was purchased from him by Edmondson in 1896.

The Limes and Fortis House estates, shown on the 1896 OS map.

*James Edmondson
(1857-1923), a keen
early cyclist.*

James Hall Renton's 1892 will named his heirs and probate was granted
in March 1895. In August 1895 the property was sold to Frederick Manson,
the lawyer who owned Wellfield and The Elms. Was he emulating the
action taken by the Somes family in 1863, buying the land to preserve the
beauty of Muswell Hill? If so, he was soon persuaded by James Edmondson
to sell it and so accept the fact that the time had come for Muswell Hill
to be developed with housing. He did well financially, for having bought
the property from the Renton estate for £19,250 he sold it to Edmondson
in April 1896 for £25,000. The sale was entered into the Middlesex
Deeds Register on 11 May 1896. Both Manson and Edmondson took out
mortgages to finance their purchases. The legal documents show that

*Parish church of
St Mary, Hornsey.*

Sleeping child, drawn by Diana Beauclerk in 1794.

Muswell Hill depicted in a nineteenth-century watercolour view.

FORTIS GREEN RD. N.

Wooden cottages in Fortis Green village.

Princes Avenue in its early days.

Queens Avenue in Edwardian times.

The post office on Colney Hatch Lane when first built.

Station Parade in former Colney Hatch Lane.

Elms Avenue in 2002.

London & Provincial Bank (now Barclays).

The Presbyterian church.

The flower stall in front of the date-stone door.

Marks & Spencer.

Martyn's interior.

*St James's after
completion in 1910.*

Congregational church.

Baptist chapel.

The Odeon cinema.

Muswell Hill Bowls Club, Kings Avenue, in 2001 – the club's centenary year.

PRESIDENT

1901	J.FOSTER.	1922	T.SCOTT FINNIE.
1902	J.E.HOUNAM.	1923	A.E.FLOYD.
1903	A.WILDSMITH.	1924	C.D.MACKAY.
1904	J.FLETCHER FORD.	1925	P.VEZEY.
1905	T.W.DAVIDSON.	1926	W.JAFFREY.
1906	G.BREWIS.	1927	G.J.BARKER.
1907	H.RANKIN.	1928	J.S.MACKIE / J.H.PARKS.
1908	W.JAFFREY.	1929	W.A.CRAWFORD.
1909	J.NICHOL.	1930	H.JUDE.
1910	J.MEDCALF.	1931	W.OGSTON.
1911	J.A.REID.	1932	W.C.JAMES.
1912	R.PULTON.	1933	A.PROCTOR.
1913	J.C.MORTLOCK.	1934	A.E.FLOYD.
1914	JOHN HYSLOP.	1935	G.SUTHERLAND.
1915	C.A.WEEDEN.	1936	G.PAIN.
1916	J.B.MATHIE.	1937	G.PAIN.
1917	A.C.HOLLINGWORTH.	1938	W.R.MEASURES.
1918	J.FARQUHARSON.	1939	P.D.TEMPEST. / G.F.FINCH.
1919	E.FLOYD / C.D.MACKAY.	1940	J.BRISBANE.
1920	DAVID HALL.	1941	G.COLES.
1921	PERCY W.RYDE.	1942	H.E.SLATER

CHAMPION

1901	C.MACKINNON.	1922	J.G.CARRUTHERS.
1902	R.PULTON.	1923	J.G.CARRUTHERS.
1903	ROBERT HALL.	1924	H.OATES.
1904	JOHN HYSLOP.	1925	J.G.CARRUTHERS.
1905	W.M.GAULD.	1926	J.S.MACKIE.
1906	A.GAULD.	1927	J.S.MACKIE.
1907	W.BROADFOOT.	1928	J.G.CARRUTHERS.
1908	A.GAULD.	1929	H.OATES.
1909	JOHN HYSLOP.	1930	J.H.PARKS.
1910	W.M.GAULD.	1931	J.G.CARRUTHERS.
1911	J.G.CARRUTHERS.	1932	J.G.CARRUTHERS.
1912	J.G.CARRUTHERS.	1933	J.FORBES.
1913	R.BROADFOOT.	1934	J.O.PILBROW.
1914	J.G.CARRUTHERS.	1935	J.O.PILBROW.
1915	J.G.CARRUTHERS.	1936	A.E.FLOYD.
1916	J.G.CARRUTHERS.	1937	J.G.CARRUTHERS.
1917	J.G.CARRUTHERS.	1938	J.G.CARRUTHERS.
1918	R.BROADFOOT.	1939	J.G.CARRUTHERS.
1919	R.BROADFOOT.	1940	G.SIMMONDS.
1920	T.SCOTT FINNIE.	1941	H.OATES.
1921	J.G.DALZELL.	1942	J.G.CARRUTHERS.

Bowls Club presidents and champions from 1901.

Cranmore Way on the Rookfield estate.

Pargetting work under the eaves.

Chester House.

Parkland Walk on the former rail track.

Stable building, Firs Avenue.

John Baird public house.

Curved shop window in Fortis Green Road.

The Grove in Alexandra Park.

Alexandra Palace on New Year's Day 2002.

250 pieces of land were sold, comprising twenty-nine acres, two roods and sixteen perches. This was the flat heartland of Muswell Hill. James Edmondson began to build a middle-class suburb with shops, churches and other amenities – the hilltop suburb that we enjoy today, over a hundred years later.

James Edmondson was one of the many unrecorded builders who built London's suburbs. Another one who was to play a large part in extending Muswell Hill was William Jefferies Collins. There was also John Cathles Hill, a local builder who was to develop housing at Crouch End, and later went on to build up the country's largest brickworks. These were family firms and operated on a larger scale than local builders who might put up just one or two rows of houses. Edmondson and Collins developed whole estates. Not only did Edmondson buy Fortis House and The Limes, he also bought the Hillfield estate opposite and The Elms and Wellfield, then he bought North Lodge. It is possible he would have purchased Fortismere and The Firs as well if Collins had not done so first.

James Edmondson's vocation in building was inherited from his father. Isaac Edmondson was a Cumberland man born in 1831 who began life as a farmer. He also ran a blacksmith's and undertook local building work. He came to London to build and by 1891 was living in Green Lanes, Stoke Newington, in a house called Woodberry Lake (Woodberry was the name James was to use for his own houses, and Muswell Hill's Woodberry Crescent takes its name from the same source). James was born in 1857 and had a sister born in 1869. He joined his father's firm, which became known as Messrs I. Edmondson and Son, Ltd, operating from No. 8 The Broadway, Highbury Park. It was a private limited company from 1906. James married and with his wife Isabelle had three sons and one daughter. Two of the sons were killed in the First World War – one in the army, one in the navy – but the firm became James Edmondson & Son Ltd. The surviving son, Major Albert James Edmondson (1887-1959) became Conservative MP for Banbury and junior government minister and was knighted in 1936. In 1945 he was ennobled as first Baron Sanford. His son (born 1920), the Revd John Edmondson DSC succeeded to the title.

The Edmondson firm built extensively in north London from Golders Green to Winchmore Hill. They also built in south London and as far afield at Westcliff-upon-Sea in Essex. Hornsey benefited from their work when in 1885 they replaced old Topsfield Hall in Crouch End (by Topsfield Parade, between Tottenham Lane and Middle Lane). The Clock Tower was to be built in front of it by a Highgate firm. Soon after the construction of Queens Parade, the first of Muswell Hill's shopping parades was erected, and it can be observed that the architectural style is the same as that of Topsfield Parade (though the other parades vary in detail). When James Edmondson began to build at Muswell Hill he established his office at No. 1 Queens Avenue (where an Edmondson manhole cover could once be seen) and then, once he had built it, at No. 6 Station Parade in Colney Hatch Lane. Ill health caused James Edmondson to move in 1923, at the age of sixty-four, to West Overcliff, Bournemouth, although without giving up his business interest. His house there was named Woodberry Lake. He died in June 1931 and was buried in Bournemouth Central cemetery. The estate office continued in Queens Avenue until the late 1920s and the firm continued beyond the Second World War, but it was then taken over and its records apparently no longer exist.

An advertisement in the *Hornsey Journal* of July 1896 announced the auction of the contents of The Limes at the end of the month, and soon afterwards the old mansion was demolished. Around the perimeter of his thirty-acre estate Edmondson was to build shopping parades, except on the north side, from where his prestigious Queens Avenue curved round to join the old road junction. Princes Avenue was laid out along the line of the carriageway leading from Muswell Hill Road (now Broadway) to Fortis House. Applications to Hornsey Urban District Council for planning permission for houses and shops began to be submitted, with council approval given in October 1896.

One notable feature of Edmondson's plans for his suburb was the width of the roads. Queens Avenue was made 65ft wide, very unusual for the time and Fortis Green Road was made 60ft wide, the latter at the request of the council. Edmondson offered to contribute £1000 to making up the road and to construct the Tetherdown portion along the line of old Tatterdown Lane.

The cedar tree on the corner of Princes Avenue.

*The former stable block
of Fortis House in
Princes Avenue.*

These widths, decided upon in the days of horse transport have become of great value in recent decades when motorized traffic has swamped the suburbs. When constructing Fortis Green Road and the parades along it, and the houses in Princes Avenue, Edmondson generously gave the space on the corner of the two for a small public open area in order to preserve an ancient cedar tree which stood in front of the now-demolished Fortis House. A part of the coach house attached to the house was also saved and forms No. 38 Princes Avenue. The grant of land (50ft 9 inches by 46ft) was made on the condition that it would be maintained by the council as a public garden forever. The cedar tree survived for some years but was removed in February 1918 on the grounds that it was a safety hazard, as by then it was dead. Replacement trees have been planted subsequently.

Edmondson obviously aimed at attracting only the best residents, for what he built were very commodious terraced houses; indeed in Queens Avenue he probably built too large as nowadays most are subdivided or used as hotels or homes for the elderly. In Princes Avenue butlers were among the servants employed. In 1899 the *Hornsey Journal* was to remark that among the hundred of houses built, or being built, there was not one suitable for a working man. It would be the inter-war years before council houses were built on the northern fringes of Muswell Hill. Houses were sold but in the Edwardian period it was still the tradition amongst the middle classes to rent or lease properties in which they lived. The quality of the suburb was also enhanced by the planting of trees by the council along the new avenues, a policy applied across the whole of Hornsey, bringing greenery to its new roads and houses, and an investment which is still enjoyed today.

For it must not be forgotten that although today we regard Muswell Hill as a place to be preserved, made a conservation area under planning law, the arrival of the town where previously there were mature trees and green lawns must have been a major change. By February 1901, the *Hornsey Journal* felt moved to comment again about Muswell Hill:

'The rush to Muswell Hill has not been quite as fierce as that to the Klondyke there being no gold there except for the fortunate owners of the land, but it has been unusually great, even for the northern suburbs. The pretty eminence has suffered an artificial cataclysm. Just as the sea nibbles gently at the east coasts and suddenly rises in wrath and carries away a sheet of it, so the suburban builder, after casting a longing eye for a few years on green fields and verdant dales at last swoops down upon them and in a few months turns them into what at first sight seem among the unlovliest products of civilisation. We must go past Muswell Hill now if we want to see grass and trees, except as something to wonder at'.

The writer is using some hyperbole here, overlooking the survival of Highgate and Queens Woods, and the acres of Alexandra Park, but one can see what he means. When countryside is turned into town the new buildings can seem unwanted and out of place. Only in time, and with a little good fortune, are they seen as good architecture and the place a community. By 1901 when the newspaper comment was made, Muswell Hill's population had risen to 5,833. In the next ten years it was to double to 11,391; the houses, as they were built, were being occupied. By 1931 the population was 16,145.

Edmondson bought Hillfield, demolished the Victorian house, and laid out Hillfield Park parallel to St James's Lane, submitting his first plans for

Hillfield Park when free of traffic.

houses in this area in 1899. His submission for fourteen sets of residential flats in St James's Lane included provision for a bicycle house at the rear – Edmondson had always been a keen cyclist. He widened the lane and at the top, fronting the road, he erected Victoria Parade in two sections divided by Hillfield Park. The remainder of this side of what is now called The Broadway remained in fragmented ownership, with Victorian villas remaining. A 1901 date stone can be seen at the bottom of Hillfield Park.

The 1900 date on the side of no. 35 Hillfield Park.

Each parade built by Edmondson was given its own name, and this was its postal address until 1961 when the council created the name Muswell Hill Broadway. Victoria Parade was on the south side between St James's church and the roundabout. On the opposite side stood Princes Parade, then Queens Parade, the latter being the first built, with the date stone 1897 still visible on its Princes Avenue flank wall (I always refer to this stone above a doorway as Muswell Hill's birth certificate). In Fortis Green Road he built St James's Parade (the name and date 1900 can still be seen) and across Princes Avenue there is Grand Parade. In what was Colney Hatch Lane (now called Muswell Hill Broadway), the parade on the left was called Station Parade (in deference to the railway station) and in 1910 Royal Parade was to be built on the opposite side, north of Edmondson's post office.

Frederick Manson must by this time have known that the old Muswell Hill had gone forever, and he sold The Elms and Wellfield estates to James Edmondson in 1899. Both these properties included land under the jurisdiction of Clerkenwell Detached which meant that Edmondson would have had to deal with two separate local authorities, Hornsey and Clerkenwell, in order to get his building plans passed. Fortunately

St James's Parade, Fortis Green Road.

Dukes Avenue.

this was not necessary. An 1899 London Government Act allowed boundaries to be adjusted. The Clerkenwell Detached area was reviewed and an assistant commissioner adjudicated that the 64½ acres should go to Hornsey. At the public enquiry J. Edmondson said that he had recently purchased a large freehold site at Muswell Hill and of the twenty acres twelve were in Clerkenwell Detached. The rental of the properties he intended erecting was from £80 to £100. The Elms estate comprised only eleven acres so his purchase would have included Wellfield.

The Elms mansion overlooking the road junction was demolished and two curving shopping parades erected and named The Exchange by Edmondson. This name is to be found in an old view of Bath House, just down the hill, as a place where coaches departed, so this old name may have been picked up and preserved instead of using a new name, say 'Elms Parade', which may not have had the right ring for Edmondson. In fact Edmondson gave the name Station Avenue to the new road he built over the Elms estate, the entrance to which was between the two new shopping parades. This he chose because the railway station was nearby, but thinking better of it he changed the road's name to Dukes Avenue, in line with his prestigious Queens Avenue and Princes Avenue. To help travellers he made a pathway between Nos 26 and 28 so that they could reach the station without having to walk up to the top of Dukes Avenue and then down Muswell Hill; the pathway still exists even though the railway station has gone.

The station proved invaluable to Edmondson's firm in its building operations. The *Muswell Hill Record*, the local paper owned by William Cummins commented:

'When building operations were in full swing, and his builders were using between 250,000 and 300,000 bricks a day, Mr Edmondson was obliged to negotiate with the railway company with a view to providing his own siding at the nearest point to Dukes Avenue. The siding was made where the footpath now leads to the station platform and Mr Edmondson had his own engine, which was used to pull the railway trucks arriving daily with the materials. This novel enterprise was favourably commented upon by the railway magazine as probably the first time that such a thing had been done by a suburban builder, and quite an American method of overcoming a difficult problem.'

On this new estate Edmondson built some of his best and most capacious houses, with fine avenues such as Wellfield and Elms. These ran north to cross the Wellfield property and join with the existing

Palace Mansions on the corner of Muswell Road.

Muswell Road, which had houses on the northern side. One of these has the name Park View as it once looked across the Wellfield and Elms estates towards Alexandra Park. The date stone, reading 1891, can be seen on a grand corner house on this side of the road; soon it would face one of Edmondson's new houses on the corner opposite, date-stoned 1905.

Lower down Muswell Road on the same side as the Wellfield estate but east of its boundary, a row of six houses had been built in 1885. These were next to the well, which still existed but was by then in a neglected state. In 1898, before it lost control of Clerkenwell Detached, Clerkenwell had proposed to buy 12ft of ground for £15, in order to preserve it. This did not go through before Clerkenwell surrendered control of building work on the land, and the well was replaced by houses. No trace of the well is to be seen at the site, and the spring water and Muswell Stream are now culverted, though its course has been traced.

On the Colney Hatch Lane perimeter of the Wellfield estate Edmondson put up Royal Parade, which extended from Muswell Road to the new postal office that he built. He turned the corner with Muswell Road with the attractive baroque-styled Palace Mansions building. South of the post office the land had long been in fragmented ownership with Castle Villas and other small properties, which were now joined on the other side by the Exchange Parade on what had been the perimeter of The Elms estate.

North Lodge had been built in the north west corner of The Limes estate in 1838 as a home for Richard Marshall's daughter Margaret when she married Henry John Smith, and stood close to Colney Hatch Lane, directly opposite Muswell Road. It was still occupied by a member of the Smith family in 1891. By 1906 Edmondson had acquired this property and had begun to build it up between 1906 and 1910. He created Woodberry Crescent there (named after his own house) and built a row of houses which he named Sunnyside (they faced east) between the two ends of the crescent as they joined Colney Hatch Lane.

In this way, by acquiring The Limes, Fortis House, Hillfield, Elms, Wellfield and North Lodge estates, Edmondson created a new suburb of wide roads, shopping parades and avenues of substantial terraced houses. Other adjacent land was acquired by other builders, notably Collins, and the suburb expanded over the surrounding green fields. Before describing these it must be mentioned that Edmondson was a man of vision, it would seem, not merely concerned with putting up houses but also foreseeing the need for social provision. He gave a site for a fire station in Queens Avenue (subsequently occupied by Muswell Hill public library); for a library in Dukes Avenue opposite the Baptist church (not taken up by Hornsey council and subsequently used as a site for a later house); and for community halls under the name of the Athenaeum (now the site of Sainsbury's) in Fortis Green Road (Edmondson was an accomplished pianist).

Church Crescent.

A practising non-conformist with a religious-minded wife, Edmondson provided sites for a Congregational church on the corner of Queens Avenue and Tetherdown and for a Baptist church in Dukes Avenue. He also sold the land for the Presbyterian church opposite Hillfield Park at a low price. Edmondson attended Highbury Quadrant Congregational church and gave liberally to Hornsey Central Hospital in Park Road, Crouch End, where he was a trustee and a governor.

Of the other Muswell Hill builders William Jefferies Collins (1856-1939) was already putting up properties in Hornsey before Edmondson arrived. The son of a successful London bookbinder, he chose building as his career and with a force of about thirty began building within Hornsey. A Baptist, he rebuilt Ferme Park Road Baptist church and in 1897 was to build Church Crescent behind St James's church on Upton Farm's former lands. W.J. Collins married a music teacher and had four sons, Ralph, Martyn, Herbert and William, and two daughters, Ada and Ethel. Martyn was killed in the First World War, but Ralph went to work for his father before moving to Southampton in 1911, whereupon Herbert and William succeeded him in the family business. Herbert was in due course to join up with Ralph to design many Southampton suburbs. In early years the firm operated from Avenue Road, Highgate.

In 1896 W.J. Collins made a major acquisition of land when he acquired the Fortismere and Firs estates that stood west of Fortis Green Road. In 1891 Samuel Somes JP had still been living at Fortismere, but with the death of Renton and the purchase of his land (across the road from Fortismere) for building purposes he must have seen that Muswell Hill's rural survival was over, and he and the occupant of The Firs moved out. Collins came to live at Fortismere and prepared plans for a new Fortismere estate in 1898, finally approved by the council in 1899. He designed Grand Avenue and five avenues running north from it, and house building had begun by 1902.

Firs Parade.

Leaside Mansion, Fortis Green.

Unlike Edmondson he did not surround the perimeter of his land with shopping parades, probably speculating that Muswell Hill would have shops enough provided by Edmondson. He did however build Firs Parade, (opposite St James's Parade) where he established his estate office. Another small row of shops called Cheapside was built in Fortis Green. Some of the perimeter of his land Collins used to build large blocks of apartments, such as Birchwood Mansions (between Firs and Birchwood Avenues) and Leaside. The drive to Fortismere House was entered from the corner of Fortis Green Road and Fortis Green, and this land was not built on until Fortis Court was erected there by the firm in around 1926. The Collins firm was also to build in Fortis Green in the 1930s, after the clearance back of Coldfall Wood allowed the laying out of Twyford Avenue, with Long Ridges (1930) and Twyford Court (1933).

Collins' developments on the south side of Fortis Green meant that the green land between Fortis Green Road and the village of Fortis Green had begun to disappear. This accelerated when the estate to the west, called Midhurst, was developed from 1903 onwards by other builders. Midhurst House was demolished but replaced by another in 1921. To the west the police station was built by 1904 on the site of the brewery, and urbanization began to be complete on the south.

Whilst designing the layout of the Fortismere estate Collins was able in 1899 to buy the twenty-three acres of the Avenue House estate on the south side of Muswell Hill. This was the estate that had been put on the market by the Clay family in 1885 and in 1891 without it being sold. As well as Avenue House it contained properties called Rookfield, Lalla Rookh, Antingua Cottage and Vale Cottage plus entrance lodges and outhouses. In 1902 Collins moved out of Fortismere, on whose lands building had begun, into Rookfield, where again he began to design new roads and to build.

Collins probably chose Rookfield rather than Avenue House to live in because it was smaller and in a better strategic location to retain as far as his building plans were concerned. It has been recorded that in the nineteenth century Muswell Hill contained a large rookery, with the birds very noisy in March when they began nesting, and the name of the house probably derived from this. In 1901 Rookfield was still occupied by A.W. Gamage, of the once-famous Holborn department store (now gone), who complained about the stench from the pond at neighbouring Lalla Rookh. When W.J. Collins moved to Southampton in around 1912 the house was still standing and put up for sale but its fate was to be demolished, and its five acres added to the Rookfield Garden estate. Avenue House and Lalla Rookh were of course demolished to allow building.

This was begun by Collins in St James's Lane and down the side of Muswell Hill. He then laid out Etheldene Avenue on the south-west side of his twenty-three-acre property and from 1906 built houses in a good conventional Edwardian style. He also sketched out a plan for new roads such as Cascade and Rookfield Avenues. From 1908 W.J. Collins began to leave the development of the Rookfield estate and the design of its houses to his two sons, Herbert and William Brannan Collins (1883-1977). It was W.B. Collins who came to dominate, especially when Herbert began to work in Southampton, and when Rookfield Garden Village Ltd was set up in 1913, W.B. Collins was the sole director.

The estate in some measure reflects the garden city idea pioneered by Ebenezer Howard and carried out by Raymond Unwin and others, with Letchworth and Welwyn Garden City the two notable expressions of the new ideas. Rookfield is not a self sufficient, mixed population place but rather a firmly middle class residential suburb conveniently near Muswell

Hill railway station for commuting into London to work. It does however have a lower density of residents, housing expressing the latest vernacular inspired architectural styles and a little, but not much communal space. The private, gated roads were undadopted by the council when laid out. Houses were rented or bought leasehold and controlled by the Collins firm. (This began to be affected by the 1967 Leasehold Reform Act; since the 1980s the estate's external appearance began to be safeguarded by an Article Four planning regulation).

William B. Collins, unlike his brother Herbert, did not have architectural training but he claimed that he had 'flair', and he did have a good aesthetic sense, which was demonstrated by his ability as a painter (he had works shown at the Royal Academy). I find the appearance of much of his housing – especially his inter-war blocks of flats – pleasing, perhaps due to his respect for the work of Lutyens. He was an important figure in the history of Muswell Hill as a built environment.

Homogenity of style between Edmondson and Collins, and by other contemporary builders at Muswell Hill, had made it a suburb of almost unique Edwardian uniformity. Unlike many other suburbs of London and other cities the roads are not lined with terraces of diverse styles but seem all to be in red brick with wooden windows, bays, porches and doors, often with pargetting in ornate style in the plasterwork in the gables. Muswell Hill was fortunate in being built at a time when the rather grim Victorian terraces of houses were being succeeded by a new domestic style which has given us, I think, some of the best domestic (and institutional) architecture of the twentieth century. It began as early as 1860 with the 'Queen Anne' style pioneered by architects Norman Shaw and W. Eden Nesfield, which in its turn owed something to the plain

Edwardian domestic architecture.

seventeenth-century English brick houses influenced by Dutch designs. This became associated with the arts and crafts movement which sought a return to traditional handicrafts (a gesture against industrialization) and to traditional vernacular building styles, methods and materials.

There emerged an arts and crafts free style, which mixed classical forms such as Baroque with vernacular detailing, freeing the domestic house from the ponderousness of the Victorian builder and improving its aesthetic appearance. Fortunately its adoption by builders at this time led to Muswell Hill being distinctly 'Edwardian' rather than Victorian. The new 'avenues' which surrounded the new shopping parades (nothing so common as a Victorian 'road' or a working-class 'street') were filled with substantial terraced houses in brick with stone dressings and white painted wood. One of the pleasures of living in Muswell Hill is in noticing the way the corners of the avenues are often turned with turrets, and how the decoration responds to the mass and shape of the building. The small-paned upper windows are a notable period detail as are the porches and balconies and other features. Inside, the houses are large and roomy and many retain attractive period features.

The builder Thomas Finnane was one of several other developers who added to Muswell Hill's built environment while keeping within the same style. Most notable is his building of Summerland Mansions and Summerland Gardens on the site of the hilltop property known as Summerlands. This was next to Belle Vue, lower down Muswell Hill, the house where Frederick Harrison had lived as a child; Belle Vue was to help supply a local need by becoming the site of a dairy depot. In front of it was built an Express tea room, its 1900 date neatly marked in plaster under the gable in period style. Summerland Mansions, which overlooks the road junction, also had its period detail in the shape of a turret roof feature, the dome of which has gone; the circular set of railings on the roof, recently restored, was once known as Maiden's Walk, a bizarre local nomenclature of no particular meaning. The building of Summerland Mansions began in 1904 and within a decade Summerland Theatre, one of the early cinema buildings, was built to its rear in Summerland Gardens.

Delaporte, a large house on Muswell Hill between St James's Lane and Alexandra Place, began in 1898 to be replaced by housing by a builder called T. Woolnough, based in Crouch End. Woolnough also put up houses in Kings Avenue, a new road that connected Edmondson's Queens Avenue with Tetherdown. The land between Queens and Kings Avenues was made available by Edmondson for the Muswell Hill Bowling Club which still operates there, having celebrated its centenary in 2001. J. Pappin, a builder based in Stoke Newington, also built houses in Kings Avenue and in Tetherdown.

Rosebery Road.

The major extension of the new suburb was to the north east on land that once belonged to the company owning Alexandra Palace and Park. Almost opposite Pages Lane an important road, Alexandra Park Road, was laid out between 1889 and 1894 and gradually built up. From Colney Hatch Lane it at first followed the line of a path to Tottenham Wood Farmhouse, which still stood at the bottom of the hill. It then curved to the east to run parallel with the boundary of Alexandra Park for some distance until it reached the Wood Green railway station on the Great Northern Railway. Houses were to be built along this road and on the land on either side.

Land on the north side of the road towards Colney Hatch Lane had been acquired in 1893 by the newly formed Muswell Hill Golf Club. A course was laid out here, extended to eighteen holes by 1895. But they gave up this land in 1899 and laid out a new links on its present site close to Tottenham Wood Farmhouse, which they used as a clubhouse from 1906 under lease from Wood Green Council. The farmhouse, dating from the late eighteenth century, was demolished in 1930 when the council decided to build a school next to it, and the golfers decided to build a new clubhouse on the links. The portico to the farmhouse remains and is a reminder of its site. The land first used as a links was then replaced by Windermere, Grassmere and Thirlmere Roads, with houses built in the first decade of the twentieth century. Known as the Lakes, the name of another English lake, Coniston, was given to the former Middleton Road on the south side of Alexandra Park Road.

On the south side a large-scale builder was Charles Rook, who erected ten shops on Alexandra Park Road which, with their 1907 date stone on the corner with Rosebery Road, remain a valuable asset for local residents, their number increased by an extension towards The Avenue, which was built in the 1930s as more houses were added to the area. Charles Rook was to build 365 houses in Coniston, Curzon, Cecil and Cranbourne Roads, in Muswell and Donovan Avenues and in Methuen Park. He built up both sides of Rosebery Road along its entire length. His own house at 33 Cecil Road, a double-fronted three-storey building, was ornately decorated with a large carved head of himself under the porch. It bears a 1903 date stone. Charles Rook died in a building accident.

Josiah Brondson was another builder, erecting houses on the south side of Cranbourne Road whilst Rook built on the north side (both builders used architects). Rosebery, Cranbourne and the other roads, all built in Edwardian style, filled the area between Alexandra Park Road and Dukes Avenue. To meet the spiritual needs of the new residents the Church of England built St Andrew's on the north side of Alexandra Park Road. At first a temporary iron church was installed, before a church designed by J.S. Alder was built, its foundation stone being laid in 1908. During the Second World War it was damaged and reconstructed in truncated form. J.S. Alder (1847-1919) lived at Hillside in Muswell Road and was a sidesman at the church. He was regularly employed by the London Diocese and was responsible for many churches and vicarages. One of his more prominent churches is St James's, Muswell Hill, which was rebuilt to his designs in the first decade of the twentieth century.

Another new road was built for Muswell Hill on the west side of the centre. This was Creighton Avenue, which in 1900 was cut through Coldfall Woods to provide a route to the old Great North Road just above East Finchley. This was still church-owned land and the new road was named after Dr Mandell Creighton (1843-1901), the Bishop of London. Creighton was an historian who had become the first professor of ecclesiastical history at Cambridge in 1894, before being made bishop of Peterborough and then, in 1897, bishop of London. He laid the

Creighton Avenue.

*Queens Parade, showing
the house that was
replaced by Lloyds Bank.*

foundation stone of St James's church not long before he died. Although at first lined with woodland, as Edwardian postcard views show, it soon began to be lined with houses, from where it connected with Pages Lane all along its length. These are quite imposing houses in size.

Muswell Hill thus came into being as a new residential suburb in the years between 1896 and about 1910. However, it still needed transport facilities and other services to make it viable firstly as a place from where large numbers of inhaitants could travel to London to work, and secondly as a local community.

CHAPTER 6

Transport and Other Needs

Middle-class residents of Muswell Hill, in the days when it was a rural village, retained business or professional interests in London and usually had a residence there as well. When they travelled it would have been on horseback or by horse-drawn vehicle, although from 1873 they had the added alternative of the branch railway serving Alexandra Palace. The residents of the new suburb were of a different order; only if they had a reliable daily transport service to take them to their place of work were they able to live six miles from London. No local industry of any significance was established in Muswell Hill to offer local employment. The new residents were commuters, apart from those in basic local services.

Transport inventions and developments had been the key to the expansion of London's built-up environment into its surrounding countryside. Some expansion had followed stagecoach and omnibus services, both horse drawn, but investment in railway construction from about 1850 onwards had had a far greater impact. Trams on rails drawn by horses, petrol buses, electric trams, London's underground railway – and later its tube system – each in turn stimulated and aided suburban expansion, as did indeed the mass manufacture of a standard bicycle.

Muswell Hill was developed when horse transport was the dominant way of getting about, apart from rail travel, and ownership of petrol-driven private cars and commercial transport had hardly begun. The branch line to Alexandra Palace was essential for the early years of urban Muswell Hill, until the arrival of the horse bus and then the petrol bus. By 1910 there were sixty-one trains running each way daily, some going to Kings Cross, some to Moorgate and some to Broad Street. The journey to Kings Cross was scheduled to take twenty minutes.

In 1902 Cranley Gardens station was added to the branch line, increasing the number of passengers. By then roads were being laid out on the south side of Muswell Hill and the new station saved walking to Highgate station. Cranley Gardens itself, on the opposite side of Muswell Hill Road from the station, was typical of the development; it had been laid out by 1894 but was only gradually built up. An early resident, Charles Landstone, wrote in his autobiography that when his family came to live in Cranley Gardens in 1907 there was only one row

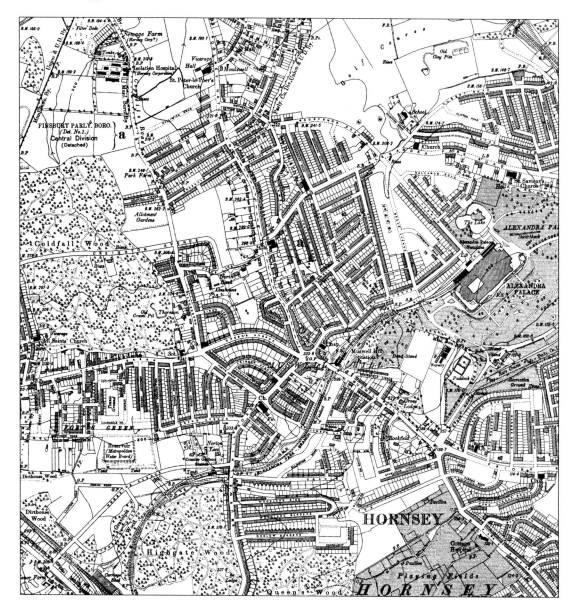

A 1920 map based on the 1910-13 survey, showing urbanization.

of houses on its mile length. They had come to Muswell Hill seeking country air; the fields had not all been built up and nearby Highgate Woods never would be.

It was not long however before the horse bus began to arrive in Muswell Hill. In April 1901 twelve horse buses commenced running between the new suburb and Charing Cross; each was drawn by three horses and made five journeys a day. The first bus provider was Mr Henry Pope, who died aged seventy-six in August 1919. Pope had premises near the Archway Tavern, at the foot of Archway Road. His new service was a one-horse bus that could accommodate twelve people inside ran from the Woodman

to the Exchange, Muswell Hill. This was to be changed in due course to a three-horse bus, which ran down Archway Road (and up its hill) to the Archway Tavern.

The arrival of a horse bus service was to leave a permanent mark on Muswell Hill in the shape of the present day roundabout filled with parked buses. The story began when it was proposed to have a 'stand' for the horse buses at the road junction. The council planned to have this on the side of the road where Summerland Mansions were being built by Thomas Finnane. Finnane objected to this and the present day roundabout can be seen as a direct result of his letter to Hornsey Council, which read:

'I understand that it is the intention to have a bus stand paved close to the footpath, and immediately opposite the shops and flats I am about to erect. May I be permitted to point out that a bus stand in that position would be very objectionable from many points of view? And considering the amount of land I am giving up for street improvement purposes I think it is only fair to have the buses moved to, say, the centre of the street. Although wishing to be reasonable as possible in every way, on behalf of my tenants and myself I must respectfully protest against this proposal.'

Finnane's protest was partly founded on the fact that in order to gain planning approval for the laying out of the 'Summerlands Estate' he had had to give up an area of land 386 feet in length and varying from sixteen feet to one foot in width for the public highway, a total area of about 310 square yards. The council gave way:

'The committee recommended that the paved stand for the omnibuses should be placed at the top of Muswell-hill, next to the Plantation, in the middle of the roadway, if the consent of the police authorities was obtained. The cost of the stand would be about £200 increasing the estimated cost of the improvement by that amount. The committee accordingly further recommend that application should be made to the Local Government Board for their sanction to the borrowing of £650.'

A photograph exists of this stand, which had been laid down by August 1902 and measured 100 feet by twelve feet. The photograph was taken when no railings encircled this area, although a set had been erected earlier it seems; the Plantation, the bosky centre island which had replaced the early village pond had always had railings of some sort round it. The photograph shows a shelter built next to the stand. This was opened in 1904 and was provided for the bus drivers, not by the bus company but by local residents out of humanitarian sympathy for the bus men. A report in *The Morning Leader* described it as 'London's First Busmen's Shelter ... the neat tiled structure cost just £80 ... the Gas Company have connected the shelter with the main free of cost ... Mr Samuel Cook of North Bank, Pages-lane, who gave largely to the funds of the shelter, opened the building'. In 1907 Hornsey Council Works Committee 'recommended the construction of an underground convenience, for men only, on the north side of the planted enclosure at the top of Muswell Hill, the estimated cost comprising seven stalls being £450'. There was long discussion before the proposal was adopted. Facilities for ladies were not supplied until 1925, and during these excavations workmen found signs of the original pond on the site.

The Exchange shops overlooking this area had opened in 1902, with Sainsbury's one of the occupiers (it was to stay there until 1966). In February 1903 a large clock was fixed above Sainsbury's, presumably as an aid both to people who wanted to catch timed buses and to the bus drivers. Unfortunately it did not survive in later years.

At this time, of course, there was no road surfacing to speak of except gravel, and mud was an inhibiting factor when using the road. Finnane's letter of protest ('very objectionable from many points of view') was no doubt referring to the stress on the road surface by the horses hooves, as well as their droppings; these two things combined made it difficult to cross roads, especially in winter, and especially for ladies wearing the long skirts of the time. For this reason setts were put into place connecting one pavement with the next, enabling pedestrians to cross the road without having to brave the mud and other undesirable features. These setts survive in many places; good examples are to be seen where Firs Avenue enters Fortis Green Road and where the northern end of Woodberry Crescent enters Colney Hatch Lane. Road sweepers were also employed. Houses would have a cross bar set in the wall by the front door so that footwear could be scraped before entering the house. In this period men wore spats, to protect their ankles and shoe tops, and gaiters were also worn by some.

Maintenance of roads was a local authority responsibility, and in order to better service Muswell Hill a sub-depot was established in 1903 in Fortis Green behind St James's school. The site was bought from the Ecclesiastical Commissioners for £5,210; the depot was to survive until the 1990s when the land was sold by Haringey Council and housing erected on the site, with a new entrance road from Tetherdown called Spring Gardens. When the depot was established there was stabling for seven horses, sheds for stores, a mens mess room and other facilities. From about 1910 Britain's roads began to be given a new covering called tarmac, an Edwardian invention. The cost of road work came from the annual

Setts to cross muddy roads.

road licence and the tax on petrol which the government introduced in 1909. In 1914 Hornsey Borough pioneered the manufacture of asphalt from clinker residue at the refuse destructor and used it satisfactorily for surfacing many miles of local roads. They also manufactured paving stones.

The horse bus had a comparatively short reign in Muswell Hill; a few years after the provision of regular services began it was replaced by the petrol bus. This was of course part of a general change in London's transport systems; in October 1910 the number of petrol buses licensed in London equalled for the first time the number of licensed horse buses. By 1912 the petrol bus had taken over on most London routes, largely due to the B-type omnibus, an improved design introduced into public service by the London & General Omnibus Company Ltd in October 1910. Certainly by 1912 Muswell Hill had a petrol bus service, route no. 4 running via Archway to Victoria station, and this was to be supplemented by a more popular route from March 1914, no. 111 from Muswell Hill through Crouch End to Finsbury Park, now served by two tube lines.

The arrival of the petrol bus in place of the horse bus was to prove a blow to the Great Northern Railway as former train passengers started to take the bus to Finsbury Park rather than the train to Kings Cross. In March 1914 the GNR survey of ordinary bookings at Muswell Hill station recorded a total of 20,051. A similar survey in March 1919 showed a total of 7,017, a remarkable drop. The GNR counter-attacked by claiming that the buses damaged their bridges at Muswell Hill and Cranley Gardens and obtained an injunction to keep down the weight and therefore the size of the buses; the General Omnibus Company responded by keeping the weight down but running more buses.

Although the petrol bus was, along with the railway train, the form of transport most used by local residents, this did not mean the disappearance of horse-drawn transport. Commercial traffic, for example delivery of goods to retailers, continued to use horse-drawn vehicles, and indeed coal and milk was still being delivered by horse transport as late as the 1960s. Petrol-driven commercial vehicles began to be used widely from the 1920s onwards as their design and capacity was improved.

Gradually the ownership of private petrol-driven cars also increased, especially among the better off, and they became more and more common in the 1920s and 1930s. Few then could have foreseen the growth in car ownership that would take place from the 1950s onwards, which would gradually increase its impact on the developed environment, especially in the 1980s and 90s, until the present situation where the number of vehicles is more than the road capacity. In Edwardian photographs the avenues of Muswell Hill always seem much wider as

Tethering ring for horses in stable yard.

they lack the row of parked cars each side of the road; the ubiquitous street-parking is one consequence of Muswell Hill having been built up in the days of horse transport, when there was no call for each house to have its own private garage. This was a development of the 1920s, as were the semi-detached houses that can be found in suburbs built later than Muswell Hill. Some houses had a building for a coach (horses tended to be kept at livery stables) but these were few in number. Stabling generally was converted into motor car storage and servicing. Birchwood Mansions, built 1907, has stabling at the rear, used by W.B. Collins himself, and this was later used for cars. When Collins built his block of Woodside flats on the corner of Fortis Green and Tetherdown in the early 1920s, he also built behind them an elegant complex of garages, based on the design of country house stable blocks; were these among the first purpose-built garages?

Delivery of goods to the shops had been provided for by Edmondson who had designed each of his shopping parades to have a service road behind it, nearly all cul-de-sacs. These mews roads sometimes had stabling in them, such as Avenue Mews between Queens Avenue and Princes Avenue. Now huge, refrigerated food-delivery vehicles of great length negotiate these service roads; Princes Lane, off Princes Avenue, is one of these, used for daily deliveries to Sainsbury's in Fortis Green Road.

Towards the end of the nineteenth century the generation of electricity to meet consumer needs slowly developed and this enabled another form of transport, the electric tram, to appear on London's streets, with power obtained through a system of overhead wires installed along its routes. In the first decade of the twentieth century this rapidly became popular as a cheap reliable way of bringing masses of people to and from their suburban residences. Some suburbs, such as Walthamstow, were developed quickly as a result, the residents being more working class than middle class. Wood Green was among the areas serviced by electric trams, which replaced horse trams in 1904. An electric tram service was to run from Turnpike Lane to the foot of Muswell Hill in Priory Road, with some single-deck vehicles going into Alexandra Park to service the Palace. Passengers alighting in the park could reach Dukes Avenue by a new path under the railway bridge. On the Highgate side of Muswell Hill a tram service was introduced along the Archway Road after the Archway bridge was widened in 1900.

Muswell Hill could have been given an electric tram service at this time. Middlesex County Council considered applying for an order from the Light Tramways Commissioners in June 1901 for a branch line from Archway Road along Muswell Hill Road to the roundabout. From there it would have proceeded down Dukes Avenue and followed a circuitous route into Wood Green. This was a further possible threat to the Great Northern Railway's passenger takings but the plans were opposed by local residents, who called a public meeting. They argued that as the vehicles travelled at up to fifteen miles per hour they were dangerous, and the proposed route was full of curves and gradients. If the rails were to be positioned in granite setts these were dangerous to horses when greasy after rain. Also, it was argued, tall trees might short-circuit the overhead cables. For better or worse Muswell Hill was never given an electric tram service. In due course, in the 1930s, trams were gradually replaced in many areas by trolley buses – commodious electric buses running on tyres and powered by overhead cables – or by motor buses, which were by then diesel driven. The route to the Palace was adapted to buses instead of trams, which had only served each end of the building separately; A through bus route was created through Alexandra Park as a result (now numbered W3).

The telephone exchange on Grand Avenue, built in 1928.

Electricity now began to be used for street lighting, though its introduction was slow as gas continued to be used in Hornsey for some time. The Hornsey Gas Company had begun to provide a street lighting service in 1869 when the area was still rural and provision was sparse. In 1903 Hornsey Council bought the North Metropolitan Electricity Supply Company and built a generating station near Hornsey railway station. Electric lighting began to be introduced into the suburban roads of the borough.

Electricity also allowed another important improvement in the shape of the telephone. This arrived in November 1907 when 'Hornsey exchange' opened in Crouch End Broadway, covering a wide area including Muswell Hill. In 1924 it was renamed Mountview, and the letters MOU followed by the individual number required had to be dialled on the circular disc on the instrument; later the name system was dropped and MOU became 340. In 1928 an exchange called Tudor was built in Grand Avenue, Muswell Hill. In the early years only a limited number of homes had a telephone installed but other users went to telephone call offices, which were usually installed in post offices, shops and railway stations. Muswell Hill's first public call office opened in the post office in Colney Hatch Lane in April 1907. Gradually telephone boxes on the pavement became common, at first in different designs but standardized in 1911 when the General Post Office took over the provision of kiosks from private enterprise. In 1918 a standard telephone box was introduced, known as Kiosk No. 1. In due course the famous red telephone kiosk designed by the architect Giles Gilbert Scott was brought into use, evolving into the classic K6 box of 1936. Whether public telephone boxes will survive the advent of the mobile phone, now owned by about half the population, is yet to be seen.

A much earlier form of communication than the telephone was to be maintained by the General Post Office in the form of the mail service. Red letter boxes were to be installed in Muswell Hill's thoroughfares, their age being determinable to a certain extent by the royal cypher on their doors. For example the post box outside St James's church has the letters VR, standing for Victoria Regina, or Queen Victoria, who reigned from 1837 to 1901. Another VR box is to be found in Pages Lane. Most other boxes in Muswell Hill date from the Edwardian period when the residential suburb was built, and bear the cypher E VII R for Edward VII Rex, who reigned from 1901 to 1910. These form one of the largest collections of Edwardian post boxes in the country. Some have been supplemented or replaced by later boxes that accompanied the reigns of King George V (1910-36), King George VI (1936-1952) and our present monarch, Queen Elizabeth II.

Mail was the means by which messages were conveyed quickly in the Edwardian era, supplemented by the telegram, which was normally used for emergencies. Compared with the deluge of often unsolicited commercial post today, levels of postal traffic were low and the sorting offices and delivery service well manned. Deliveries as late as 9 p.m. by hardworking postmen carrying all their mail in sacks on their backs meant that in most cases an item posted in the morning would reach any English destination the same day. Muswell Hill residents would have used this quick way of communicating. Another useful development was the postcard. When the new streets were built itinerant photographers with plate cameras took photos of them and sold them in quantity to householders through shops. Use of pictorial postcards had been facilitated by the relaxation of postal regulations which allowed $5\frac{1}{2}$ x $3\frac{1}{2}$ inch cards with a picture on one side and an address on the other to be sent with an halfpenny stamp. Consequently there was a boom in sending picture postcards with short messages about returning home safely, or arriving soon, or 'this view shows our new house', many of which have fortunately survived, which is to the benefit of local historians as they show places as they once were. Unfortunately they have since the 1970s become a target of collectors and often command very high prices. Today picture postcards seem largely to be used by holidaymakers and sent from abroad.

In the absence of broadcast radio and television, news was primarily communicated by national newspapers, supplemented by local weeklies. William R. Cummins was an important local figure in this field as far as Muswell Hill was concerned. He had come to the hilltop in 1896 as a teenage newspaper boy, selling papers each day near The Green Man, and was to be a successful local businessman, with newsagent's and stationery shops at No. 5 The Exchange, at the top of Dukes Avenue (the shop still

HORNSEY'S CHOICE.
1910

AS WE GO TO PRESS WE HEAR THAT MR. D. WHO HAS LEFT HORNSEY (TO LORD RONALDSHAY) HAS RECEIVED 20,647 PROMISES FOR THE NEXT ELECTION ON ACCOUNT OF THE ADMIRABLE MANNER IN WHICH THE LAST ELECTION WAS CONDUCTED BY HIMSELF & FRIENDS

HORNSEY DIVISION OF MIDDLESEX.
GENERAL PARLIAMENTARY ELECTION, 1910.

RONALDSHAY. **U.** 12,014.

DUMMETT. **R** 8633.

MAJORITY
FOR TARIFF REFORM. **3381**

DUMPER DUMMETTS BOOM.
COOK (R.E.N YES! I AM IN THE DUMPS AS THEY SAID I WAS SURE TO GET IN. MY FRIENDS DID ALL THEY COULD TO HELP ME, BY DISTURBING AND BREAKING UP TORY MEETINGS, MAKING UNTRUE ACCUSATIONS, SNEAKING ELECTION BOARDS, MUDSLINGING, HOOTING, PENSION, BREAD & HORSE FLESH LIES, RADICAL NEWS RAGS AND FINALLY "JEFFERSONS WEEKLY SCRIBBLE" IN THE B.P.
I'M LEAVING THEE IN SORROW HORNSEY. I'M LEAVING THEE IN TEARS. **FAREWELL.**

Lord Ronaldshay wins his Parliamentary seat in 1910.

bears his name), and at No. 21 Station Parade, Colney Hatch Lane. In 1907 he started up a local paper called the *Muswell Hill Record* and in 1915 he founded a printing works for it on Muswell Hill Broadway, in premises located near the rear of Crocodile Antiques. Letter writing was more common in the days before the dominance of the telephone and in due course Cummins owned several retail stationery businesses, as well as two florist's shops and a nursery of over one acre. Cummins used to go to Fleet Street in the early hours of the morning to collect national newspapers and in 1906 he was able to bring the parliamentary election results to Muswell Hill, to a waiting crowd of some 4,000 people. He was thanked by the Earl of Ronaldshay for bringing news of his re-election as Conservative MP for Hornsey.

The *Muswell Hill Record* survived for some fifty years but one that survives to this day is the *Journal* which began in 1879 as the *Seven Sisters and Finsbury Park Journal*. By the time it moved to 33 Crouch Hill in 1885 it had become the *Hornsey and Finsbury Park Journal and North Islington Standard*. Later it moved to premises in Tottenham Lane, Crouch End, and in the 1990s began issuing different editions for each local area, including one for Muswell Hill. This practice was also adopted by the *Hampstead & Highgate Express* with an edition called *Broadway* covering Muswell Hill, Crouch End and Hornsey. This paper seems to have begun in 1860 and been owned from 1862 by George Jealous, who also founded the *Journal* but sold it in 1884.

Advertisements featured in early newspapers and could also be seen on local billboards and hoardings, which were not then subject to today's planning constraints. An interesting wall advertisement can still be seen on the side of Victoria Parade closest to Marks and Spencer; it reads 'Army Club cigarettes 30 1/- 10 for 6d' and has probably been there since the 1930s, at times protected by a hoarding over it. Planning regulations in the conservation area now require that it be uncovered, although a half-size hoarding sits above it and graffiti is an ever-present menace though their shop has closed.

This advertisement is on the fragmented south-east side of what is now Muswell Hill Broadway, where there were once separate housing sites with Victorian premises between Summerland Mansions and Victoria Parade. The offices and printing works of the *Muswell Hill Record* were then at Nos 18 and 19 Broadway, Muswell Hill Road, for the name of Broadway existed in Edwardian times for this short stretch of premises. At No. 16 Broadway was the builders' merchant's Bond and White, whose products had been essential to the building and decoration work carried out on Muswell Hill's houses. The history of this firm is told by Joan Schwitzer in *Hornsey Historical Society Bulletin No. 20*, published in 1979 to mark the firm's centenary. It began in 1879 when local builder and decorator Charles White set up a business. In 1900 he went into partnership with a James Bond, although in 1909 Bond severed connections and went to Buckinghamshire. The White family expanded the firm successfully; in 1913 H.E. White rented a one-storey shed next to an old domestic building on the Broadway, and when in 1927 this large house was demolished to allow Lloyds Bank to put up their bank on the corner of Summerland Gardens, Bond and White followed suit and erected a brick building on their site for their sales shop. The lease of this ran out in 1970 and Bond and White sought to renew it but were unable to, and so moved instead to a shop in the Odeon complex in order to remain in the centre of Muswell Hill. Their old shop became Budgen's supermarket and was then converted into Marks & Spencer, who also expanded into the surviving pair of adjacent Victorian villas, the lower floors of which had become shops. Bond and White had established a large depot for their materials on a site acquired in 1916 by Queens Wood, and this still functions.

The local authority role in providing the sinews and services for the suburb was of course pivotal. Building controls, road layout, road surfacing and tree planting, refuse collection, street cleaning, street lighting and power supply have already been mentioned. To these must be added the provision of recreation facilities; as well as Alexandra Park and Queens Wood there were other pockets of land and Coldfall Woods became a council responsibility. Add also libraries (though Muswell Hill had to wait until 1931 when the Queens Avenue building was opened),

A Borough of Hornsey (BH) hydrant cover from 1905.

education (an elementary school was opened in 1913 near St James's Lane, followed by Coldfall School in 1928) and in due course municipal housing with the provision of the Coldfall estate on the north side of Muswell Hill in 1924-26.

Provision of these local authority services was aided by Hornsey becoming a borough instead of an urban district in 1903, a reflection of the size of its population. It sought to increase this municipal borough status to county borough status (with responsibilities matching that of a county), but failed to do so. However it had been only the second municipal borough to be formed in Middlesex when this status was granted in 1903. As a borough it had a mayor and, from 1907, thirty councillors and ten aldermen (a post that no longer exists). In 1910 Muswell Hill ward had three councillors, two of whom lived in Dukes Avenue and the other in Queens Avenue, the latter being the mayor, Councillor Alfred Yeatman. Despite strong Liberal representation (which often meant non-conformist) the council was to be dominated by Municipal Reformers, later Conservatives. The borough collected the forerunner of council tax, called rates, which in 1902 stood at seven shillings in the pound, that is, for each pound of the assessed value of the property, the owner would pay seven shillings.

The local authority also aided the maintenance of health within the borough, which it described in its guide as 'Healthy Hornsey', probably a reflection of its many open spaces, its distance from London and its hilly nature and abundance of trees. It paid particular attention to schools, introducing the teaching of personal hygiene in 1904 and the medical inspection of school children in 1905. A borough campaign tackled food hygiene. Infectious diseases such as diphtheria and scarlet fever were targeted and maternity and child welfare services provided, including dental treatment at welfare centres.

Law and order was the responsibility of the Metropolitan Police, which in 1840 had established a police station in Hornsey, staffed by four police sergeants and eighteen police constables. From these Muswell Hill was allocated one sergeant and six constables, and in 1904 was provided with its own police station in Fortis Green, a building which still stands. Costing £5,570 it had stabling for six horses.

CHAPTER 7
Places to Meet

The importance of the shops in Muswell Hill cannot be overestimated. In late Victorian times, when the population was comparatively sparse, there were a few near The Green Man (a general shop on one side of the road and a fishmonger's and a tobacconist's on the other) and a post office in Colney Hatch Lane. Edmondson provided eight parades, Collins one more and Finnane another, each with around twenty shops. This tight core of shops in the centre, in a U shape, made a focus for the residents in the surrounding avenues and still does today, perhaps the reason why so many local people think of Muswell Hill as a village; a similar situation exists in Crouch End. This central core is not overwhelmed by a transport complex. The continuance of small specialist shops also evokes the earlier times of local traders, though the presence today of chain businesses such as Sainsbury's and Marks & Spencer adds to rather than detracts from its appeal as a shopping centre for food and small household items. There are suburbs and suburbs, some just vast housing estates with no lively shopping core, but Muswell Hill is distinct from these due to its parades. It is like a village high street.

Queens Parade, between Queens Avenue and Princes Avenue, was the first to go up and to open for business. A 1913 street directory shows us the goods and trades that the early shops offered. On the corner of Queens Avenue stood Manor Farm Dairy, selling dairy produce from local farms surviving in Finchley and north of Muswell Hill. Down the parade from it were a baker's, a boot manufacturer's, Madame Rutherford, sellers of robes; Maltby & Son, described as oil and colour men; a chemist's, a maker of artificial teeth, a branch of Home & Colonial Stores (once a well-known grocery chain), the Domestic Bazaar Company, a butcher, a provisions dealer, a draper, a milliner and a branch of the dyeing and cleaning firm Eastman & Son, also once well known. Next to this was Martyns, which was there from the beginning and has survived to this day. Now run by the grandson of the first shop owner, Martyns' interior is a delight, as is the smell of its roasting coffee. Following on towards Princes Avenue were a ladies' outfitter, a confectioner, then a branch of W.H. Smith newsagents (still surviving). Then there was a fishmonger's (later this was to be Macfisheries), the boot and shoe firm Lilley & Skinner, a bookseller's, and on the corner a

wine shop called Findlay, Mackie, Todd & Co.; a wine shop still occupies these premises.

In Victoria Parade on the other side of the road were two other shops that were to survive until the 1980s or 90s: Carpenters the ironmonger's shop, which occupied two lots of premises on the corner of Hillfield Park, and in the same block, nearer St James's Lane, a butchers called Pulham & Sons. The latter was distinguished by good tiling (in common with many butchers), as was the branch of Friern Manor Dairy Farm at No. 13 Victoria Parade. On the opposite corner of Hillfield Park to Carpenters was a branch of the London Joint Stock Bank; this fine corner building with its dome still survives, by descent now occupied by a bank called HSC (Hong Kong and Shangai Bank). Another early bank building that has survived is Barclays on the corner of Queens Avenue; this began life as the London and Provincial Bank and was completed in 1898, with a corner entrance door.

In the banks, shops and post office, local residents would meet, chatting with neighbours, members of their church, parents of children at the same school, drinkers at the same pub or shoppers at the same store, developing a community sense through grumbling at local nuisances shared, possibly the failure of the local authority to maintain streets, or the quality of goods purchased. What were these churches, schools, entertainments that local people shared?

Edwardian Muswell Hill, a place of respectability in a time of a firm temperance ideals, had churches of many denominations, as did other London suburbs. A 1903 survey carried out for the Nonconformists by Richard Mudie Smith and the Daily News, using 400 well-supported enumerators, checked on the churchgoing habits of Londoners. The survey showed that out of London's 6,240,336 inhabitants only a fifth attended church, despite widespread church and chapel provision. Of these, 538,477 were Anglican worshippers, 545,817 Nonconformists, and 96,281 Roman Catholics.

In Muswell Hill, at the Anglican church of St James, the congregations recorded for 1903 were 677 at morning service and 419 at the evening service. This was comparable with the Congregationalists, who had 603 in the morning and 568 in the evening. Presbyterians had 489 in the morning and 328 in the evening, while Baptists recorded 314 in the morning and 370 in the evening. So on a 1903 Sunday the total Nonconformist attendance in Muswell Hill was greater than that for the Church of England (1096 for the C of E and 3,326 for the four Nonconformist churches). The figures suggest that the religious affiliations of the new residents were already established.

What church buildings did local residents use and how did they come to be built? St James's church has, of course, the longest history, having been established in 1842 on its corner site, with extensions in 1874. A church council was formed in 1896 to consider what steps should be taken to provide for the growing parish. By this time the church had structural problems and when church architect J.S. Alder (who worked for the London Diocese and was to live in Muswell Road) was called in he virtually condemned the building, a view endorsed by a second architect. A public meeting decided that Muswell Hill needed a new church 'built on improved and modern principles', which would accommodate between 900 and 1,000 worshippers. The competition for its design was won by J.S. Alder. Fundraising was successful and building work began, with the foundation stone laid in 1900 and the church consecrated in 1901. Completion, with tower and spire, took until 1910. The top of the spire is 179ft high, on a spot 337ft above sea level, making the church a notable landmark.

A church hall to aid the social life of the church took longer to achieve. A site was acquired in Fortis Green Road in 1911, but with the intervention of the 1914-1918 Great War the hall was not built until 1925. This handsome building, still in use, was designed by George Grey Wornum, the architect of the headquarters of the Royal Institute of British Architects in London's Portland Place. Absence of a purpose-built church hall had not, however, deterred parishioners from social activities. When for fundraising purposes they staged a musical tragedy about the Maid of Muswell Hill, they staged it in the large hall of St James's Church School.

Four Nonconformist churches were built in Muswell Hill: the Congregational church on the corner of Tetherdown and Queens Avenue, the Presbyterian church on the Broadway opposite Hillfield Park, the Baptist church in Dukes Avenue and the Wesleyan Methodist church on the corner of Colney Hatch Lane and Alexandra Park Road. All are on prominent sites, all except the Baptists on the corner. This accorded with thinking amongst Nonconformists at the time. In a 1901 book about building Nonconformist churches written by the architects Joseph Crouch and Edmund Butler, it is argued that the time for building in back streets had passed. Nonconformity was a power in the land and it was important for the New Church to be in a leading thoroughfare, if possible on a corner site; the lighting is more easily managed, the book argues, and the church has a commanding position. A modified form of Gothic style was recommended and the churches were not to be weak copies of Anglican models.

The Presbyterian church certainly seems to accord with these recommendations. It has a corner site with Princes Avenue and is in an Art Nouveau version of Gothic, built with white flints and hard Ruabon brick. It has a tower and spirelet and is so prominent that it was once called 'the nose on the face of Muswell Hill'. When built the interior

had a raked, semicircular seating design to seat 1000 people. It is an attractive building of great character, and can be seen and appreciated from Hillfield Park opposite, possibly a piece of town planning devised by Edmondson when his firm came to divide their two sections of Victoria Parade shortly before the church itself was built.

The origins of this site and church go back to 1896 when Edmondson acquired the Fortis House and The Limes estates. The Church Extension Committee of the London Presbytery became aware of this development and in 1897 the committee's convenor, Sir George Barclay Bruce, purchased this central site with his own money. He leased it to the newly-formed congregation for a nominal sum and advanced the money for the building of a church hall that would serve as a temporary church. Designed by Arthur O. Breeds, building work began on the hall in 1898, opening in November of that year. A minister was appointed and fundraising for the new church started, with sales of work and a three-day bazaar, the latter including a ladies nail-driving competition, recital on an Edison phonograph (recorded sound had arrived in England for the first time) and a trained American duck.

Five architects entered the competition to design the Presbyterian church, and this was won by George and Reginald Baines who had recently designed the Baptist church in Dukes Avenue. George Baines (1852-1934) was articled in Great Yarmouth but won a competition early in his career to build a Baptist chapel in Accrington and set up his practice in that south Lancashire town before moving to London in 1884. He took his son Reginald into the business in 1901 and designed over 200 church and school buildings, as well as stores, factories, a model village for Messrs Chivers & Sons and blocks of flats in Westminster. Baines had originally intended the Muswell Hill church to be built with light yellow brick from Costessey near Norwich, but delivery problems made him chose instead the hard, red, Welsh brick which has apparently weathered well. Baines built an almost identical church in Braemar Avenue, Wood Green, using the same materials.

The Presbyterian church foundation stone (on the Princes Avenue side) is dated 1902, and the church opened in 1903. The Breeds building at its rear was then used as the church hall, a gathering point for Muswell Hill residents. The Presbyterians gave up their church in 1972, when they amalgamated with the Congregationalists to form a United Reformed Church and it was decided that the building would be sold and the congregation would use the Tetherdown church. Threatened with demolition, local protests led to a Grade II listing and a public enquiry leading to the saving of the chapel. Plans to use it as a concert hall failed and it was turned into offices, which the staff did not find very satisfactory as a place of work, the tenants being Haringey

Council's housing department. After standing empty for a time it was converted in 1997 into a public house, which it still is today. The hall behind was turned into flats. The original Presbyterians, with their temperance views, must be turning in their graves but at least a fine Muswell Hill building, now over 100 years old, has been saved.

A small Congregational gathering had begun locally in the late nineteenth century, with worship taking place in the Muswell Hill drawing room of a Holborn solicitor before a site for an iron church was acquired opposite Pages Lane on Tetherdown in 1891. The congregation embraced Baptists as well but unfortunately the Union Church was weakened by personality clashes. Fortunately these were resolved and revival ensued with Edmondson's generous donation of a portion of his newly acquired land for a church on the Tetherdown Queens Avenue site in 1897. The architect chosen was Percy Morley Horder (1870-1944), son of William Horder, the Congregational Minister at Wood Green. Horder was only twenty-eight when he designed Muswell Hill Congregational church. He dressed stylishly for the time in a cape and broad hat, but was said to be puritan in character. He was to build other Congregational churches in Leyton, Hackney and Bowes Park. Building of the Muswell Hill church began in 1898 to his designs, formal consecration took place in May 1899 and it opened for public service on May Day 1900. With some modifications (such as the porch) it still operates over a century later, its acoustics making it well suited to the musical events that are held there.

Presbyterian church.

For social purposes a separate church hall seems essential, but like the Church of England, the Congregationalists had to wait until after the First World War to achieve such a building. Fortunately a site was secured directly opposite the church in Tetherdown. It was designed by church member and architect Stanley Griffith and built in 1928-29; recently its fine brick appearance helped it win listed status. Today it forms a useful meeting place for many Muswell Hill groups, and is hired out constantly, having taken on greater importance since the demise of the Athenaeum. Halls play a vital role in community life, providing a venue for drama groups, political meetings and jumble sales; a community without one is diminished – Edmondson saw this when he gave Muswell Hill the Athenaeum halls.

Similarly the hall beneath the Baptist church in Dukes Avenue is now becoming more widely used for public meetings. This hall in some measure owes its existence to George Baines, the architect chosen to design the church building. He suggested that as the site was sloping and the church had to be built on piers, these should go deeper in order to provide space for classrooms and a hall under the church. Above it was built an auditorium seating about 750, with a gallery that was curved

Wesleyan Methodist church.

instead of straight-fronted to echo the style of the Queens Hall, the famous concert hall north of Oxford Circus where the Proms began. The building is in red brick and is another Baines excursion into a free adaptation of Perpendicular Gothic. The interior is little altered and is distinguished by an early ventilation system.

The creation of this Baptist church was due to the Reverend W.J. Mills, vice-president of the London Baptist Association and in due course the first Muswell Hill pastor. Mills went to see the lie of the land in Muswell Hill as the new suburb was being built. A report on the laying of the foundation stone in the *Hornsey Journal* in 1901 quotes Mills saying that when he and a fellow Baptist minister visited James Edmondson in his Queens Avenue office, Edmondson promised that if they were prepared to build a church, then he was prepared to give a freehold site for the purpose. Edmondson pointed out to them a suitable site for their chapel. According to the account in the *Journal*: 'They took the liberty of suggesting a more public site was desirable. Mr Edmondson then took them around the estate and then came to the spot on which they stood (at the foundation stone ceremony) which was formerly occupied by an old mansion and said if you like the site you are welcome to it.' It was thus that the Baptist church stands at a more prominent spot than it might have done. Its spirelet can be seen from the Broadway and adds much to Muswell Hill's townscape, as does Baines's Presbyterian church. In each case the granting of the site was due to Edmondson's generosity. He was not a Baptist himself but his wife was and it was she who laid the foundation stone, as a glance at it shows. Erection of the building was not by Edmondson's firm either but by Mattocks, at a cost of £6,408 16s. The stone was laid on Mrs Edmondson's birthday, the date having presumably been chosen specifically for that purpose.

The Baptist church opened in 1902, the congregation having previously met in Norfolk House School in Muswell Avenue. W.J. Collins, Muswell Hill's other major developer, donated £200 to the cost; after the laying of the foundation stone in 1901 he had invited guests back to Fortismere House (then still standing) in Fortis Green Road for a garden party. Again the local church became the centre of social activity, hosting a literary society, a ladies' meeting, Boy Scouts and Girl Guides – who used the church gymnasium – a Sunday School that soon attracted 190 members and the Girls' Guild of Help, aimed mainly at girls in domestic service.

Weslyan Methodists in Muswell Hill began to meet in the late nineteenth century, at first in private houses such as Essex View in Colney Hatch Lane – an 1840s villa that had fine views across to Essex before building began opposite (it is now called Alhabama); then in Tottenham Wood Farmhouse, which was occupied by William Russell, one of the Alexandra Estate Company's bailiffs; then in the Norwegian Chalet, which stood at the foot of the wide avenue leading up to Alexandra Palace from Alexandra Park Road. A site on the corner of Colney Hatch Lane and Alexandra Park Road was then purchased for £400 and a church was designed by Josiah Gunton, a Methodist. This took five years to build before it was finally completed with its corner tower and chancel. It was open for worship from April 1899. In 1901 the Methodists began to use the iron chapel belonging to the Congregationalists in Tetherdown as a Sunday School, but later they constructed a purpose-built Sunday School, designed by architect Arthur Boney, adjacent to the church. This Sunday School pioneered grading and proved be a successful institution. The iron hall was then set up in Pembroke Road, a turning off Colney Hatch Lane to the north, as a Mission Hall where it survived until the 1990s.

The Edwardian period saw the first provision in Muswell Hill for Roman Catholic worship since the Middle Ages. In 1903 an order of nuns of St Martin de Tours were effectively forced to leave France (among other Catholic teaching orders) and were encouraged to settle in Muswell Hill by Finchley Parish priest Father Powell. First they moved into Newport Villa in Tetherdown, and soon Mass here was attended by some forty or fifty Catholics. Then in 1907 they moved into Springfield House in Pages Lane, which became their convent. The nuns opened a school, building an extension to the eastern side of the house, where Mass began to be held.

In 1917 Father Powell moved into Oncot, a villa in Colney Hatch Lane next to Pinner Lodge at No. 3 (which still survives). In 1920, while he was living at the villa, a temporary church was built at the rear. Although he died in 1928 at the young age of sixty (the dampness of Oncot being partly blamed for his ill health), plans to build on the site continued, with Oncot being demolished and a presbytery (1930) and a church (1938) being built. Designed in Byzantine style by architect T.H.B. Scott, the church seats 600. Social life centred around the church, and also around the school that the nuns had built by extending Springfield House. The convent was to survive until 2000 when Springfield was sold and converted into apartments. From 1959 the school, with additional buildings, became part of the state system for infants and juniors. Our Lady of Muswell church and school take their name from the chapel on the nuns' medieval farm.

The Athenaeum.

The Society of Friends, or Quakers, also began to hold meetings in Muswell Hill, some in the Athenaeum. However, in 1926 a house was acquired in Church Crescent and converted into a meeting-house. Again, this hall has proved useful as a meeting place for local organizations, especially since the loss in 1966 of the Athenaeum.

Edmondson reserved a site for this Athenaeum next to his St James's Parade in Fortis Green Road, and from 1900 erected a Classically-styled building with pediment and two domed towers with rusticated arched frontage onto the street. A glass canopy was added. Inside were two halls, seating 466 and 200 people, and other rooms. The building was used at different times for a conservatoire of music, a girls school (from 1910), a cinema (1913–1936) and a debating society called the Muswell Hill Parliament. It was also used for religious purposes, not only by the Society of Friends but also by a Spiritualist church and as a synagogue. A shop on the street at the front was occupied by a commercial photographer.

The name 'Athenaeum' is not so familiar nowadays but in Edwardian times was more so. It derives from the Greek word for the temple of Athene, goddess of wisdom, and was given to several literary or scientific buildings. The most famous survivor is the gentleman's club off Pall Mall, built in 1830 by the architect Decimus Burton. The demolition of the Muswell Hill Athenaeum took place before conservation legislation was brought in and only the corner building survives, leading into the culs-de-sac called Athenaeum Place. The site was taken by a block of flats, with Sainsbury's supermarket at ground level. For sixty years the Athenaeum had been a focal point for Muswell Hill's social life, used by many organisations, and its loss has meant a search for alternative venues. Edmondson had originally had it erected in order to raise the status of his new suburb, and doubtless because he also foresaw the need for a community centre.

Other provision and venues for entertainments were to arrive in the developing suburb. Behind Summerland Mansions was some empty space, and there the Summerfield Theatre was built in Summerland Gardens. A surviving September 1913 brochure indicates that the area was used as a pleasure garden in the tradition of London precursors like Vauxhall, Highbury Barn or Cremorne, with different programmes of music offered on Thursdays, Fridays and Saturdays, and was lit up in the evening with thousands of fairy lights. The ground sloped and was probably not at that time considered for building. Inclusive admission to the gardens and the theatre in 1913 was sixpence.

The 1913 brochure tells us that the films shown in the theatre on Thursdays included a vitagraph drama called *His Life for His Emperor* and the comedy *Heart of a Doll*. In 1916, according to an advertisement in the *Muswell Hill Record* for the Muswell Hill Electric Theatre, Hall Caine's

SUMMERLAND
CINEMA, MUSWELL HILL. N.10.
Proprietor : ARTHUR FERRISS.   Resident Manager: EUSTACE GEO. HASTING.
Telephone - - - - - TUDOR 5831.

ATHENÆUM
PICTURE PLAYHOUSE, Muswell Hill.
Proprietor : MR. ARTHUR FERRISS.   Resident Manager: MR. PERCY WALLIS, M.C.
Telephone - - - - - TUDOR 5831.

Continuous Performance 2.30 p.m. to 10.30 p.m.   Saturdays a

Saturday, March 30th	Saturday, March 30th
Monte Blue in "Brass Knuckles" Tim McCoy in "Law of the Range"	John Gilbert in "Man, Woman and Sin" George Lewis in "Honeymoon Flats"

MONDAY, APRIL 1st, for THREE DAYS

Q SHIPS
The Story of the British Mystery Ships.

Virginia Lee Corbin in "SHORT SKIRTS"

MONDAY, APRIL 1st, for THREE DAYS

POLA NEGRI, WARNER BAXTER & TULLIO CARMINATI in
THREE SINNERS
From the Play "The Second Wife."

Dorothy Gish, Will Rogers & Nelson Keys in "TIPTOES"
From the West-End Stage Success.

THURSDAY, APRIL 4th, for THREE DAYS

MYRNA LOY in
THE CRIMSON CITY
Mystery of the Orient.

Dolores Costello in "TENDERLOIN"
An Underworld Romance.

THURSDAY, APRIL 4th, for THREE DAYS

MARION DAVIES AND CONRAD NAGEL in
QUALITY STREET
From the Famous Play by Sir James Barrie.

Viola Dana & Ralph Graves in "THAT CERTAIN THING"
A Lesson on Love's Funny Side.

Week commencing April 8th	Week commencing April 8th
Harold Lloyd in "Speedy"   Lois Wilson in "Coney Island"
Stewart Rome in "The Ware Case" Louise Fazenda in "Ambitious Annie"	Norma Shearer in "The Latest from Paris" Harold Lloyd in "Speedy"
Jack Holt in "The Vanishing Pioneers"

Printed and published by the Proprietors of the "Muswell Hill Record and Friern Barnet Journal," W. R. Cummins, Limited, at 18
Telephone, Tudor 4649.   Branch Office: 19, Grand Parade, Friern Barnet, N.12

Cinema advertisements, March 1929.

masterpiece *The Eternal City* was being shown three times daily at 3.00, 5.30 and 8.00 p.m., with prices of admission at one shilling, sixpence and threepence, with children under twelve going half price. Being shown on other days were two 'official war films': 'Ypres', and 'The Prince of Wales in the Front Line'. Coming soon was Mary Pickford in a four-part *Mistress Nell*. Seats could be booked in advance at no extra charge. This early cinema was to survive into the thirties, but programmes seem to have ended after 1936 when Muswell Hill acquired two modern cinemas, the Odeon and the Ritz.

Films could also be seen at Alexandra Palace from 1911 to 1914, where they made a profit; these screenings were not resumed after the War, during which the government took over the building, using it at first for Belgian refugees and then for imprisoned aliens. The building was not handed back to the trustees until 1922. A connection was made between Muswell Hill and the early cinema industry when the British pioneer filmmaker Robert Paul opened one of the UK's first film studios in Sydney Road in 1899. Surviving Paul films show scenes shot in that area.

Alexandra Palace and Park conveniently offered Muswell Hill residents a variety of entertainments, not least the horse racing meetings held on the track in the park. This was a comparatively prosperous period for this huge complex, which was now under municipal control. Fireworks, fairs, circuses, outdoor and indoor events of all kinds were to be seen. Crowds came to watch people parachuting from balloons, particularly Dolly Shepherd. This local girl had begun as a waitress but had been invited by Captain Auguste Gaudron, a French aeronaut at whose table she had waited, to become a female parachutist. Garbed in a suitable, self-designed knickerbocker suit she began to make jumps, a career she was to follow across the country with great success from 1903 to 1912.

In 1935 the palace was chosen by the British Broadcasting Corporation as a suitable venue to begin making regular television broadcasts to people's homes, so pioneering a new entertainment medium. A plaque on the wall commemorates the date of the first transmissions: 2 November 1936. This had meant the BBC rebuilding the south-east tower and putting a transmission mast on it, and inside creating two studios, A and B. One was used by John Baird for his earlier mechanical form of broadcasting, and the other by Marconi-EMI. After six months of trials it was the latter, electronic system that was chosen. Initially only two hours of transmission were programmed and this could only be seen within a radius of about 25 miles. But from this limited beginning was to emerge the dominant world-wide form of entertainment that we know today. Alexandra Palace's pioneering role in this great development has been given scant regard; however, the two original studios have survived various threats to redevelop them and perhaps one day they will form the core of a museum devoted to television's technical history.

The Edwardians of course were unaware of the coming delights of the domestic television screen. Even radio broadcasts were unknown to them, as these did not emerge until after the First World War when the crystal receiving set began to be acquired. Regular broadcasting of radio programmes began in Pittsburgh, US in November 1920, and with the formation of the British Broadcasting Company in 1922, the first UK broadcasts began in November of that year. Electronics manufacturers then began to manufacture and sell radio sets and in 1927, when the British Broadcasting Company became the Corporation, transmissions started to be run on public service lines, taking regard of the public's information, education and minority cultural needs. Broadcasts became

The proposed licensed hotel opposite the Congregational church.

an addition to domestic life and a new entertainment in the home, rather than outside, became available.

There were still many attractions outside of the home though. The feel of a glass in the hand and good company in the ambience of a public house was not to disappear, but in Muswell Hill the spreading of such establishments was held back by the strength of the Temperance movement, which opposed the building of new public houses. Edmondson, for example had wanted a licensed hotel on the corner of Queens Avenue and Fortis Green Road and he built an impressive pillared building there. He was thwarted by Temperance opposition led by the Congregationalists, opposite whose church the hotel would stand; ironically he had given them the site for the church. So Edmondson did not built a new public house or hotel in the new suburb and neither did his fellow non-conformist W.J. Collins. Muswell Hill men (women might have wanted to go too, but it was not considered 'respectable' for ladies to enter pubs) wanting to have a social hour in a bar had the choice of The Green Man or the tiny Royal Oak in St James's Lane, which was the meeting point for the 'villagers' living nearby. Alternatively, they could walk to Fortis Green and visit the Clissold Arms or The Alexandra. For the discerning, the Princes Club opened in a building at the junction of Princes Avenue and Avenue Mews, where no doubt thirsts could be quenched. It was to survive until 1999.

Another place for Muswell Hill men to gather together was Muswell Hill Parliament. This seemingly now-forgotten society was one of at least half a dozen in the country (another was at Hampstead) which followed the procedures of the House of Commons to debate political issues. In the 1920-21 session, for example, it debated 'the excessive rates in local boroughs', measures for dealing with unemployment, the appointment of a Public Defender, and proportional representation. Members represented constituencies, had party allegiances and were supervised by a speaker, and there was also a mace. It originated in 1908 and met at first in the Athenaeum, then in the Presbyterian hall, and then in Tollington school hall. In 1948, while at the school hall, it was televised by the BBC. It ceased to meet in the 1950s, probably a casualty of changes in methods of communication when political debate shifted from packed local halls to the television screen and the radio broadcast.

Women were probably a minority in Muswell Hill Parliament, if they attended at all, but would have built up their own network of personal friendships and arranged domestic meetings such as dinner parties. In Edwardian days many would have had the assistance of live-in or other servants, or domestic help of some kind at least. Advertisements for such workers can be seen in the small advertisement pages of the *Muswell Hill Record* and other local papers. It was the Second World War between

1939-45 that made servants scarce, a change from which social lives of the middle classes never fully recovered. The rooms that had been the servants' quarters were adapted to other purposes.

In the first decades of the twentieth century, unless they were very poor, women did not go out to work once they were married; their jobs were given up automatically, this being the rule within many organizations, for example the Civil Service. Salary levels for women were of course lower than for men doing the same job, as the man was automatically seen as the chief wage earner and supporter of his family. But for middle-class women in a suburb like Muswell Hill there was scope for other activity, not least furnishing and running a commodious home. Apart from the local shops the suburban housewife had easy access to the great department stores of the West End: Whiteleys, Harrods, Dickens & Jones, Marshall & Snellgrove, Swan & Edgar, Debenham & Freebody, Liberty's, the Army & Navy, the Civil Service Stores, John Lewis, Arthur Gamage, Burberry's, Waring & Gillow, John Maple and Selfridges, all of which offered various delights in rebuilt Edwardian stores. Jones Brothers of Holloway was nearer and delivered to Muswell Hill.

Children and their upbringing was another major concern for many women. State-supported provision was limited to St James's Church School for infants and juniors and later a similar new state school that was erected in Alexandra Place in 1913; this latter was seen as a temporary building, its metal exterior earning it the name the 'tin' or 'tinpot' school. Despite this it was to continue in use until the late 1960s, when it was replaced by the building erected on the former railway near to where the station had been.

Middle-class parents thus sought out private schools in the locality, either boarding schools or day schools. One of the earliest, catering for juniors, was Norfolk House School, built in 1897 in Muswell Avenue, which in 1908 claimed to be the only purpose-built school out of seventeen then existing. The school also catered for older girls and had a school of domestic science at 11 Alexandra Park Road, where boarders were received. Other private schools included the Brakespeare House day and boarding school for girls at 30 Muswell Road; Highfield day and boarding school for boys and the Cranley House day and boarding school for girls, both of which were in Muswell Hill Road, where Kings House school for girls was also located. The latter was run by Miss Lear and its pupils were known as Cordelians. There was a modern school for girls and kindergarten at 2 Queens Avenue (established 1898) and the St Margaret school for girls at 11 Queens Avenue. Others existed as well; it is hoped that a research project will catalogue all of them in due course.

A surviving brochure for Highfield School, which stood on land that since 1928 has been occupied by a telephone exchange, shows a wide

Miss Broad, who was headmistress of Tollington Girls' School in 1928.

range of subjects on offer and states that the curriculum is intended to 'give a thorough grounding in all essentials of a good education, preparing the pupil for a business or professional career'. It had a laboratory, a gymnasium and adjacent sports ground. Fees for day pupils were up to three guineas a term and for boarders from twelve guineas a term upwards according to age. This was probably one of the better local schools, and it survived until 1925.

Another was Tollington Boys School, destined to be bought in 1919 by Middlesex County Council and developed as a state grammar school. It was established in Tetherdown in 1902 when the proprietor William Campbell put up a purpose-built school in the front garden of his villa, Thorntons. William Campbell was the son of the original founder who had established a school in Tollington Park, Islington, and this branch was opened to catch the new middle-class market that had opened up with the creation of Muswell Hill as a suburb. Tollington Girls School was to follow, opened in 1911 in Grand Avenue; from 1958 this building was to become Tetherdown infant and junior school.

Among the church schools was St Aloysius in Highgate, catering for Roman Catholic boys. The more prestigious Highgate School in the village was a minor public school with boarders and day boys. Stationers School in Crouch End was another school of good standing, founded by the City livery company of the same name.

Library provision in Muswell Hill was not made until 1931 when the public lending library was opened in Queens Avenue on the site of the former fire station, Before then scholars and readers would have had to travel to Highgate to find a public library, one having been built in Shepherds Hill in 1902, designed by Hornsey Council engineer, Edwin J. Lovegrove. Highgate library had a stock of 400 volumes when it opened. Private lending libraries were available, such as the Royal Library operating at 18 Queens Parade, as were nation-wide services like Mudie's Lending Library. Lending libraries were also established in branches of Boots the Chemist and W.H. Smith, the newsagents and book sellers. These were to persist until the 1950s when cheap paperbacks made them unviable. Before then, for a few people at least, suburban respectability made a book borrowed from Boots preferable to one borrowed from a public library.

Provision was not lacking for sporting activities. A private Muswell Hill Bowls Club was established in 1900 in grounds off Kings Avenue made available by Edmondson. Muswell Hill Golf Club offered membership at stiff fees to both men end women, with women making up a third of the numbers. Tennis courts could be found in the Fortis Green area and at Alexandra Palace, where the young could also enjoy roller-skating. In Alexandra Park there were both football and cricket clubs with pitches. Bowls also took place in the park, and indoor bowling in the Palace itself from Edwardian times. The lake in the park was in due course to be used by fishing enthusiasts.

Thus from its inception Muswell Hill became not just an empty suburb but the focus of a community, with churches, schools, entertainments and provision for sports. It also had its ring of green space from Highgate Woods to Alexandra Park. From the beginning, for the middle class at least, it was a success.

A W.H. Smith lending library plate, stamped December 1919.

CHAPTER 8
The Edwardian Suburb Survives

It has been the fate of many towns and suburbs to be thoroughly changed by later generations. This was particularly so before the 1960s when a conservation movement changed attitudes (and legislation) towards period buildings. Muswell Hill has managed to avoid large-scale destruction, and much of it has Conservation Area status and protection, so that the Edwardian-built environment remains largely untouched despite the passing of a hundred years. The main exceptions are a number of Victorian properties and undeveloped sites.

For example it was the undeveloped Coldfall Wood which was largely lost in the 1920s. Hornsey Borough sought to remedy the shortage of housing for the less well-off in the area by building the Coldfall estate on former woodland north of Creighton Avenue. A grid of five roads with 412 terraced houses was laid out in 1924-25 and a school and a Church of England church provided. The council set aside thirty-four acres of woodland to remain free from development and north of this are playing fields and a large cemetery reaching to the North Circular Road (built in around 1929). South of Creighton Avenue W.B. Collins built Twyford Avenue in the style of the Rookfield estate and lined Fortis Green with the Twyford Court and Long Ridges blocks of flats in the 1930s. The north side of Fortis Green thus became urbanized, like its south side.

Twyford Avenue.

Twyford Court, built in 1931.

Building of flats was not favoured by Hornsey Council in the 1920s and the developer who proposed building Dorchester Court on the north side of Muswell Road at its junction with Colney Hatch Lane in 1927 was only given planning permission on the condition that he limited it to four storeys. By the 1930s when it was built, massive blocks were being built further up Colney Hatch Lane in the shape of Barrington Court, St Ivian Court, Cedar Court and Seymour Court. It was the early Victorian villas that had lined the west side of Colney Hatch Lane north of Pages Lane that were destroyed in order for these to be built. Among those to go was The Thatched House, a notable mansion once occupied by a City auctioneer, which had stables and grazing in the fields behind, now covered by the houses of Pages Hill and Pages Lane.

A more notable block of flats built in Pages Lane in 1937 was Whitehall Lodge. This tall white block is in the 'international modernist' style of the time, echoing Highpoint, the celebrated block built at Highgate. It was a Victorian building, not an Edwardian one, which was lost to allow Whitehall Court to be built; this was the group of almshouses built in 1861 for Madame Uzcielli.

The 1920s and 1930s were a period of rebuilding near the centre of Muswell Hill. In 1927 Lloyds Bank replaced an old house on the corner of Summerland Gardens, with Bond & White rebuilding on the adjacent side, then in 1936 the Odeon complex was erected in Muswell Hill Road on the corner with Fortis Green Road. Again it was not Edwardian but Victorian houses that were demolished when seven out of the nine 1880s houses built opposite St James's church were sacrificed in order for the cinema, shops and flats to be built. Now listed Grade Two Starred, the Odeon is seen as the great masterpiece of the cinema architect George

Dorchester Court.

Coles. The entrance foyer is skewed round in relation to the auditorium due to opposition from St James's church to having the cinema entrance directly opposite (cinema going was not quite respectable in some people's eyes, even in the 1930s, the era of building big cinemas). In 1936 another cinema called the Ritz (later the ABC) was also built at the top of Muswell Hill, on a site occupied by a garage next to the railway. Unlike the Odeon this was not to survive, despite being designed by another famous cinema architect called W.R. Glen. It was replaced in 1978 by a tall brick office block with penthouses.

St James's Lane was also the scene of changes in the 1930s, as is recorded in a 1934 issue of the *Muswell Hill Record*:

> 'The old village of Muswell Hill which is situated in St James's Lane is rapidly disappearing and quite three quarters of the old cottages, the majority of which are 160 to 170 years old, are now standing empty awaiting demolition…to make way for modern flats which are to be built on the site… The only relic will be the quaint old public house, The Royal Oak…'

Whitehall Lodge.

Among the new blocks of flats was Vallette Court, which replaced twenty-six cottages. These were improvement schemes by the council to upgrade old housing.

Another new council building was the public library opened in 1931 in Queens Avenue and built to the designs of the borough engineer W.H. Adams. It is now a listed building. Formerly on this site was the fire station building of 1899 for which Edmondson had provided the land; from 1926 this had been in use as a Highways sub-depot, and was seen as

North Bank, with the church attached.

expendable. In 1936 the Post Office added a new façade to their building, which had been built by Edmondson in Edwardian times; until covered up by Post Office signage in the 1980s it bore a date stone and a GVR cypher above the windows (King George V died in January 1936).

In 1934 the owner of the Grove Lodge estate on the side of Muswell Hill planned to develop it with housing, but fortunately this did not take place. It has become one of the two surviving early estates in the area, the other being the North Bank estate in Pages Lane. The latter owes its survival principally to Harold Guylee Chester (1887-1973) who bought it in 1924 and gave the house and grounds to the Methodist Church, who have left it undeveloped (except for some residential homes for the elderly) so that it forms a green lung in the middle of Muswell Hill. Chester was also responsible for the survival of the early nineteenth-century villas at Nos 3, 5 and 7 Colney Hatch Lane adjacent to North Bank, which he also owned. No. 7 remains in the occupation of the Methodist Church and Nos 3 and 5 are privately occupied. No. 9 also belonged to Chester and was called Devonshire Lodge. In the 1950s he gave this to the Church as a site on which to build a youth centre and hostel. When this was built – in 1959-60 to the designs of architect Charles Pike – it was named Chester House.

Having survived the rebuilding of the 1930s the Edwardian fabric of Muswell Hill had then to survive the bombing that took place in the 1940s during the Second World War. Bombs were to fall in Collingwood, Leaside, Firs and Queens Avenues and elsewhere, and some post-war rebuilding was inevitable. The major casualty was St James's church, which was burnt out by a firebomb on 19 April 1941; it has however been restored. Another bomb landed on St James's Parade at the corner with Princes Avenue. This remained a bombsite for over ten years until 1959

*A V1 bomb falls on
Fortis Green, 26 July
1944.*

when Muswell Hill gained a new pub with the building of the John Baird on the land. The name is a tribute to the television pioneer who worked at Alexandra Palace in 1936.

The disappearance of canvas pullout shades over shop windows was just one of a number of subtle changes to the appearance of the shopping parades as the decades have gone by. Fortunately, conservationists have managed to get shopkeepers to take pride in the curved window framing in Fortis Green Road and most of these have been freed from fascia encumbrances. Codes exist to guide shop front designers to keep within Edwardian styles, but these are not always followed. Latterly a joint partnership scheme between Haringey Council and English Heritage was developed to preserve Edwardian features, and period lamp standards, for example, have been installed.

Expansion of schools provision was to be another feature of the second half of the twentieth century. Muswell Hill junior and infants school was built in the 1960s on the side of Muswell Hill adjacent to the pedestrian entrance to Alexandra Park. This was possible because in 1954 passenger services ceased on the branch railway to Alexandra Palace. Electrification of this line, which would have become part of the Northern Line system, was almost complete in 1939 when war broke out, and when the war was finished the investment was abandoned. The out-of-date steam train system became unviable and the line closed to become, for most of its length between Muswell Hill and Finsbury Park, a linear park known as the Parkland Walk. Land at the side of Muswell Hill was used for the new school after the station was demolished in 1960.

Broadway shops in the 1950s.

Another school which expanded over previously undeveloped land was the one now known as Fortismere in Tetherdown. This grew out of the former Tollington School, which merged with the William Grimshaw Secondary Modern School in Creighton Avenue to become Creighton Comprehensive School in 1965. In 1983, with falling school rolls, this amalgamated with Alexandra Park Comprehensive School and was renamed Fortismere School. It has expanded with new buildings and playing fields on the former Hornsey Common and Coldfall Woods land, so helping to preserve open land.

St James's School also took advantage of the land released by the closure of the Palace branch railway when it built new premises in Woodside Avenue where the track had been. The Victorian and later school buildings in Fortis Green were demolished in 1968 and the block of residential flats now known as Spring House was built on the site. Next door a former fire station was replaced by a medical clinic now to be replaced by flats.

Though these site use changes and redevelopments occurred in the 1960s and 1970s, since then the major change has surely been the outstanding growth in motorized traffic. Not only have parked cars transformed the appearance of Muswell Hill's avenues, the road improvements designed to help the flow of traffic have included traffic lights, islands, pedestrian crossings, road markings, bus lanes and the ubiquitous traffic warden. This, more than anything else, has altered the leisurely ambience favourable to the pedestrian which the Edwardian suburb enjoyed when it was first built.

However, not only has the Edwardian period fabric of Muswell Hill largely survived despite the stress of modern motorized transport demands,

*Alexandra Palace
Station, with a steam
train.*

but so also has its social structure. The large houses lining the avenues command high prices and there has not been an overwhelming amount of sub-division of them into separate flats, though this has occurred to some extent. The 1981 Census showed that the Muswell Hill district was favoured by the self-employed and by supervisory economic groups; immigrants tended to be from places other than the New Commonwealth. Out of a population of approximately 29,000, the majority commuted elsewhere to work, some 40% travelling by car. (As in earlier decades, there still is very little industry in the area other than some small craft and light industrial concerns.) Most local employment was in shops, offices and local government, including education and civic amenities. If there has been any noticeable change in the makeup of the middle-class population of Muswell Hill then it has been towards a greater proportion of people working in the media and entertainment fields, especially in television, a development it shares with neighbouring Crouch End where a recording studio has helped attract international figures in the world of popular music. Notable local celebrities have included Rod Stewart, The Kinks, Peter Sellars, and Maureen Lipman, who has featured Muswell Hill in some of her humorous books.

Fame of another kind came to Muswell Hill when in 1983 a Haringey Council worker called to deal with a blocked drain at a Cranley Gardens house uncovered human remains. As a result Denis Nilson was sentenced to life imprisonment for six murders carried out between 1979 and 1983. As with the famous 1896 murder this drew spectators to the area for a while.

Muswell Hill is not without crime but the incidence of it is no higher than in other suburbs, and perhaps is lower than in many. Licensed bars behind The Green Man at the top of Muswell Hill, in the converted Presbyterian church, now a pub, and in two other establishments, draw young people to the area and sometimes rowdiness can occur. But in

Fortismere School.

Fortismere School grounds.

general the ambience of Muswell Hill continues to be respectable and quiet. In daytime it is never without a flow of shoppers, aided by half a dozen or more bus routes which pass through it, connecting with tube stations at Highgate, Bounds Green and Finsbury Park. St James's and other churches draw good congregations and schools such as Fortismere are popular with local residents, who have to compete for the limited number of school places available for their children.

So the hilltop inheritance of Muswell Hill as a desirable place to live, close to trees and open spaces and with a variety of outstanding views to enjoy, continues from one generation to the next. Long may it continue.

Walking Tour

The walk begins in the Edwardian heart of Muswell Hill and then becomes an anti-clockwise circular tour taking in surviving nineteenth-century properties located north of Muswell Hill Broadway. This is all on the flat land on which the suburb was developed. Further routes are then suggested which necessarily take in the hilly terrain that makes Muswell Hill so distinctive.

> **Start at St James's church at the junction of Muswell Hill Road with Muswell Hill Broadway.**

Built between 1902-10 this magnificent church in the Perpendicular style, in Bath and Ancaster stone, replaced an earlier (1842) church on the site. The present building was designed by church architect J.S. Alder. Standing at a point 337ft above sea level, its tower and spire reach to 179ft, so making it a prominent local landmark. Bombed and gutted in April 1941 it was restored in 1952. The vicarage is behind the church in St James's Lane.

> **Walk across the pedestrian crossing to the shops and cinema opposite.**

The Odeon complex, opened in 1936 and comprising shops, flats and cinema, replaced a late Victorian terrace of houses and is one of the few post-Edwardian structures in the heart of Muswell Hill. The cinema is considered to be the finest Odeon designed by architect George Coles and is Grade Two starred, largely because of its Art Deco interior. Look across to Sainsbury's. This tall 1966 building is another intrusion, replacing a Classical-style concert hall building named the Athenaeum built from 1900 by James Edmondson, a man who played the largest part in developing the Edwardian suburb. It was the location of a school, clubs such as Muswell Hill Parliament, and entertainments such as a cinema. To the left notice the lettering 'St James's Parade 1900' above the shopping parade, one of the eight major parades built by Edmondson to provide a central core for the suburb. To the right, starting at Athenaeum Place, is Princes Parade.

*Walk across the pedestrian crossing to Princes Parade
and follow it as it turns out of Fortis Green Road onto
Muswell Hill Broadway. You are now in the heart of the
Edwardian suburb. Walk forward away from St James's
church until you reach Princes Avenue on your left.*

On the corner is the former Presbyterian church, now converted into
a public house. Its 1902 date stone can be seen in Princes Avenue.
Designed in Art Nouveau Gothic style by architect George Baines,
its flint and hard red Ruabon brickwork has weathered well. It
became redundant in 1972 when the Presbyterians joined up with the
Congregationalists and moved to their church in Tetherdown. It was
listed and saved from demolition after a public enquiry. For a time it
was used for offices. A distinctive feature of the Broadway, it has been
described as 'the nose on the face of Muswell Hill'. Look across the
Broadway to the gap formed by Hillfield Park to see the fine view of
London. On the other side of Princes Avenue from the church notice
the date stone 1897 above a doorway – this marks when Queens
Parade, the next line of shops, was built. This was the first parade
erected by Edmondson and the stone can be regarded as Muswell Hill's
'birth certificate'.

Stop by Martyn's grocery shop. This is a family business that has traded
here since the parade was built; the smell of grinding coffee makes it
particularly attractive during the day. Across the road Lloyds Bank was
built in 1927, replacing a nineteenth-century house, whilst Marks &
Spencer's food store next to it occupies a brick building that once housed
local building firm Bond and White. There is also the remains of a pair of
Victorian gabled houses. At the end of the parade turn left into Queens
Avenue. Muswell Hill public library on the left-hand side was built in 1931
on the site of a small former fire station of 1899. It was designed by Hornsey
Borough engineer W.H. Adams and is now listed. Queens Avenue, laid
out in 1897, was deemed by Edmondson to be his most impressive avenue,
with an unusual width of 65ft and very large houses, some of which are now
hotels. In some of the front garden walls can be seen carved stone pieces
from The Limes, the old house that once stood here.

Walk across the pedestrian crossing to Barclays Bank.

Notice the granite water trough in Queens Avenue. This once stood
in the roundabout area and was provided, along with many others, by
the Metropolitan and Cattle Trough Association in the days of horse
transport, mainly for the benefit of horses and dogs. The Barclays

Walking Tour

building was erected in 1898 as a branch of the London and Provincial Bank. Stand by the pedestrian railings and look towards the roundabout: the shops on the left, divided by Dukes Avenue, which joins the roundabout area here, were built in 1900 by Edmondson and named The Exchange. They replaced a mansion called The Elms, the ivy-covered front façade of which faced towards the roundabout area. Across its grounds Edmondson laid out Dukes Avenue and other connecting avenues, building fine domestic architecture in long terraces; these properties now command high prices. To the right of The Exchange shops is the top of the steep road called Muswell Hill, a very ancient route from London which continued to the north. Near its top, on the left, is the renamed Green Man – an alehouse is reputed to have stood here since Tudor times, serving travellers. Next to it from 1873 to 1960 stood Muswell Hill railway station on the line to Alexandra Palace; the track is now the Parkland Walk. The tall red-brick office block opposite The Green Man was built in 1980, replacing a 1936 cinema which had opened as the Ritz, to become the ABC before its demolition in 1978. The Village bar and restaurant, originally built in Art Nouveau style and dating from 1900, was once an Express Dairy tea room with a milk depot behind it. Next to it stand Summerland Mansions, built from 1904 by Thomas Finnane. When from 1901 onwards a horse bus service began to terminate at Muswell Hill, it was planned to erect a bus stand directly outside these mansions. Mr Finnane's objections, accepted by Hornsey Council, led to the stand being positioned in the centre of the road junction, which until 1858 had been the site of the village pond. This explains why the roundabout is now occupied by buses, an unusual feature in an urban area. A circular walk can be taken around the roundabout to look at these buildings, but crossing the roads is hazardous so it is not included in this guided tour.

> **Turn left, keeping to the same side as Barclays Bank, past the road sign reading '1-353 Muswell Hill Broadway' and walking forward with shops each side of the road.**

This stretch is the southern end of Colney Hatch Lane, and that name is resumed further on. Renaming by Hornsey Council in 1960 was part of a strategy to do away with using individually named parades in postal addresses, the idea being that this would aid deliveries. The shops on the left, built by 1900, were named Station Parade by Edmondson. Opposite are some fragmented non-Edmondson properties, among them the former Castle Villas, which date from the first half of the

nineteenth century, the front gardens now occupied by single-storey shops. North of them, was Woolworths, now a 99p store, then the post office, erected in 1902 by Edmonds but refaced in 1936 (its date stone and GVR cypher are now obscured by Post Office signage). The parade of shops beyond it was appropriately named by Edmondson as Royal Parade.

> **Walk forward beyond the shops on the left to reach Woodberry Crescent.**

This crescent was laid out by Edmondson from 1906 on the site of North Lodge. It is named after Edmondson's own house. Where the further, other end of the crescent meets Colney Hatch Lane there is a line of sets, or stones, from one pavement to the other. This was to allow pedestrians to cross in the days before tarmac road surfaces when it could be muddy. Royal Parade opposite terminates at Palace Mansions, built in a Baroque style. This building is on the corner of Muswell Road, which was once a footpath leading to the well from which Muswell Hill took its name. The well was built over by 1900; a plaque on No. 40 Muswell Road marks its site. It was on land given to Clerkenwell nuns in the twelfth century by the Bishop of London, who was then lord of the manor of Hornsey. The well was reputed to cure illnesses and it became a place of pilgrimage. It continued to supply water to local villagers until the arrival of piped water. Dorchester Court on the other corner of Muswell Road was one of the several 1930s blocks of flats built in Colney Hatch Lane to replace villas.

> **Continue forward on the left-hand side of Colney Hatch Lane.**

On the left the Roman Catholic Church of Our Lady of Muswell was built in 1938 to the designs of architect T.H. Scott. It replaced a villa named Oncott, which was numbered 1 Colney Hatch Lane and was one of a row of early nineteenth-century villas on this side of Colney Hatch Lane. Nos 3, 5 and 7 have survived, but those further north were replaced in the 1930s by large blocks of flats. Survival was due to ownership by Lloyds underwriter Guy Chester, who gave property to the Methodist Church. He also owned No. 9, called Devonshire Lodge, which stood on the corner with Pages Lane, but which was given to the Methodists by Chester to enable a national Methodist headquarters and youth hostel to be built; this was erected in 1959 to the designs of architect Charles Pike and named Chester House. The Methodist

Walking Tour

church once stood on the other side of Colney Hatch Lane, on the corner with Alexandra Park Road. Erected in 1899, this was demolished in around 1983 due to structural faults and replaced by a block of flats.

> **Turn left to walk along Pages Lane on the left-hand (south) side.**

Pages Lane, which was once quite narrow, was an old rural back lane connecting Colney Hatch Lane, the medieval route to the north, with another northward route, now called Tetherdown but previously Tatterdown Lane. Past Chester House is a surviving nineteenth-century villa called North Bank, which is typical of pre-Edwardian Muswell Hill. It was purchased in 1924 by Guy Chester and given to the Methodist church and developed as a youth centre. The undeveloped acreage (except for housing blocks for the elderly at the southern side) provides a green lung and access is usually possible; the wooded area contains a chestnut tree some 350 years old. North Bank, which replaced an earlier house, now has a new Methodist church attached to its east side, the replacement for the Colney Hatch Lane building. Dating from 1984, it was designed by Peter Knollt and Chris Lelliot. Just past North Bank stands Whitehall Lodge, another of Muswell Hill's more modern buildings, built in 1937 on the site of Victorian almshouses. Its style echoes that of Highpoint at Highgate, which was built just before by Lubetkin in the Modern European style of the 1930s. Next to it is Our Lady of Muswell Primary School, recently reconstructed. Part of the building was an extension of the convent next to it where the nuns had run a private girls' school before the primary school replaced it in 1959. The nuns occupied Springfield House, an early Victorian property that still stands beyond the school. The convent was closed down in 1999 and Springfield House has been converted into three separate houses (for sale at the time of writing at an asking price of £795,000 each). Opposite, on the corner with Tetherdown and Coppetts Road, is a row of 1870s cottages, with a further terrace to the rear. Small, semi-detached villas from the same period are in Coppetts Road. This corner development was once known as Tatterdown Place and provided housing for artisans and the like.

> **Turn left into Tetherdown and keep to the left-hand side.**

Just past the corner shops, 80 Tetherdown has a plaque to the writer and poet W.E. Henley (1849-1903) who lived in an uncompleted public house on this site in 1896-98. His most famous lines are 'I am the master

Walking Tour

of my fate, I am the captain of my soul' and 'My head is bloody but unbowed'. Opposite once stood Muswell Lodge, the site of the famous 1896 murder of the elderly occupant, which drew so much attention to Muswell Hill. That side of Tetherdown was once Hornsey Common, with Coldfall Wood beyond it to the west, and was not built upon before the 1860s. Just past No. 80 are some 1930s houses, built on the site of former greenhouses. Number 72 was the first house owned by Peter Sellers, the Goon and film actor. On the opposite side is Muswell United Synagogue, with its 1965 foundation stone. Next to it is the Muswell Hill branch of Tollington School, a private school built onto the front of a former villa by the school owner in 1901, which became a leading local boys school; it is now part of Muswell Hill's leading comprehensive school, named Fortismere. Cross by the pedestrian crossing leading to the main gates of Fortismere School and turn left. On the right stands Tetherdown Hall, with a 1928 date stone on the south side, and beyond it a block of flats called Woodside, built by William B. Collins in the 1920s on the site of a villa of that name . A path between the two leads to a well-designed set of garages, modelled on stables and dating from the 1920s.

On the opposite side of the road from the hall stands the United Reformed church. This was built as the Congregational church in 1897 to designs by Morley Horder, a 28-year-old architect. The corner site was given by Edmondson. On the opposite corner of Queens Avenue are Queens Mansions, dated 1901. The building on the corner of Queens Avenue and Fortis Green Road was intended by Edmondson to be a licensed hotel but the temperance movement prevented it being established.

> **Cross from Woodside Flats at the traffic lights to Fortis Court opposite.**

Fortis Court stands on the corner of Fortis Green Road with Fortis Green. It was built by William B. Collins in the 1920s on a site that was formerly the drive of Fortismere House, an old villa which had been purchased by the Collins family and its grounds used to built the Fortismere residential estate. Look down Fortis Green Road towards St James's church: the land on the right was developed by Collins, whereas the land on the left was developed by Edmondson. On the right in Fortis Green Road, just past Fortis Court is St James's church hall, built in 1925 to the designs of George Grey Wornum, later the architect of the Royal Institute of British Architects (RIBA) headquarters in Portland Place W1. Across Birchwood Avenue stands Birchwood Mansions, built by Collins in the Edwardian period. It is a good example of restrained Arts and Crafts architecture concealing the bulk of the building.

Walking Tour

Walk past it and turn right into Firs Avenue.

On the right is a converted stables enclave; a tethering ring is still there. Return to Fortis Green Road and cross to the small corner garden. This was given to the council by Edmondson so that a mature cedar tree here could be preserved. The tree was in front of Fortis House, demolished in 1896 for redevelopment, but the first property in Princes Avenue (No. 38) is a modified part of the mansion's coach house, which was retained. On the opposite corner stands the John Baird public house, named after the television pioneer who worked at Alexandra Palace. It was built in 1959 on a bombsite. Continue down this side of Fortis Green Road, noting the curved tops to the shop windows, and on the other side of the road in Firs Parade (built by Collins), one or two elegant half shops with curved windows. You are now back at the start of the walk.

For a further tour, this time over hilly terrain, walk down St James Lane by the side of St James's church.

As you descend, enjoy the fine landscape view ahead. The railway viaduct over the road was built in the 1870s and carried the line to Alexandra Palace. Passenger services ceased in 1954 and the track is now a parkland walk. On the left, beyond the bridge, is the Royal Oak. The current building replaced a small weather-boarded pub of the same name in 1965. Where St James's Lane is was once the location of a rural hamlet; the cottages were set on the side of Muswell Hill Common, which lay to the left. Valette Court, next to the pub, was built in 1934 to replace twenty-six of these cottages. Continue down St James's Lane on the right-hand side until the lane turns to the left, almost at a right angle. Nos 108 and 110 in this corner are surviving early rural houses, and No. 112 is labelled 'Manor Farm Cottages 1903'. Go through a passageway by No.108 and you will find yourself in the Rookfield Garden Estate. Some fifteen acres of land once belonging to the Avenue House estate were developed here by the Collins family on garden city lines from Edwardian times onwards, a development contemporary with the suburb of Hampstead Garden. If desired the estate can be explored at leisure. To continue the walk turn left along Cascade Avenue, noting the house styles and retention of trees and green space. The exit from the avenue onto steep Muswell Hill is gated. Turn left, then left again back into St James's Lane. Note on the right-hand side the surviving weather-boarded house at No. 103,

*Walking
Tour*

a reminder of earlier rural times. Retrace the route back up St James's Lane to the viaduct bridge. A return can be made to St James's church and the Broadway from here or alternatively a longer walk taken to visit Alexandra Palace…

Go under the bridge and ascend the steps on the left up onto the viaduct.

This is the parkland walk along the former railway track. The viaduct is an impressive piece of Victorian civil engineering, with seventeen arches used to carry the line across this valley to the high position occupied by Alexandra Palace. Turn left. From a little further along on the right can be seen a magnificent view over London to the south. At the end the walk goes under a road bridge. At the end turn right and walk up the slope to the entrance to Alexandra Park, using a footbridge. This brings you into The Grove, once the grounds of an estate of the same name, which was acquired in 1863 to form part of the new park. The mansion was demolished when the railway was built.

Walk down the path on the left, which takes you through the grounds, with a café on the left. Look across to the lawns on the right and to an avenue lined with trees. This is known as Dr Johnson's walk as the famous English literary figure visited this estate with some of his famous contemporaries in the eighteenth century, when it was occupied by Topham Beauclerk. At the end of the path, passing a small car park on the right, you come into the main part of Alexandra Park with Alexandra Palace on its eminence to be seen opposite.

Walk up to the Palace. The first set of main doors leads into the Palm Court, which was remodelled after the 1980 fire with a fine glass roof. To the right is the Phoenix bar where refreshments can usually be obtained. The palace is used as an exhibition centre, a location for conferences and other events, and for private entertainments such as banquets. Exit again and walk to the left onto the south terrace, which offers one of the best views of London anywhere. Continue to the far end where a blue plaque can be seen denoting that this was where on 2 November 1936 a regular television service was inaugurated, providing programmes for domestic receivers. In 1935 the British Broadcasting Corporation had leased this end of the palace, erected a mast and created two television studios within the palace to try out both the Baird and the EMI-Marconi systems. From these beginnings came world-wide television. Another plaque commemorates the internment in the Palace during the First World War of German civilians that had been resident in the UK when the war began. Continue to the left to the entrance of the ice-skating rink. Enter

Walking Tour

the foyer to see another fine, restored glass roof. Ice skating can usually be glimpsed through the glass doors; it is a popular venue both with children and with ice-hockey teams.

> **Retrace your route back to the small car park and exit under the railway arch along a path leading into Dukes Avenue.**

Turn left and walk uphill back to Muswell Hill Broadway. Here you will pass fine Edwardian domestic architecture with good period detail. There are other good examples of such on the turnings on the right, such as Elms Avenue and Wellfield Avenue. This estate was developed by Edmondson. On the left, near the top, is the Baptist church, built from 1901 onwards to the designs of George Baines, architect of the Presbyterian church in the Broadway, on a site given by Edmondson. Its spirelet, which is visible from the Broadway, is an attractive feature. The walk now terminates in the Broadway.

Two other Walks that can be taken are firstly to explore Highgate Wood and Queens Wood and secondly to look at Fortis Green village.

> **From St James's church, cross to the Odeon complex and then turn left to walk down Muswell Hill Road, which heads to Highgate Wood.**

The road leads downhill and reaches Woodside Avenue on the right. Walk down this avenue a few yards to see the first house on the right called Norton Lees, a private mansion built in 1875. This now forms part of St Luke's Woodside Hospital, established here in 1930. The branch railway to Alexandra Palace used to run on the opposite side of Woodside Avenue, where the St James's School buildings and the residential building for the elderly were built in the 1960s in place of Cranley Gardens railway station, which opened in 1902 but ceased to operate in the 1950s. The land on the left-hand side of Muswell Hill Road was once Upton Farm. Continue on the right-hand side until you reach Highgate Woods. These can be explored at leisure, and contain a refreshment pavilion. By the side of the entrance to the woods is the entrance to a section of the parkland walk; a return to St James's Lane can be made along this. Queens Wood is on the opposite side of the road to Highgate Wood and can also be explored.

From St James's church walk up Fortis Green Road to the traffic lights. Turn left and walk along Fortis Green.

The Gables block of flats (to the left) built by Collins is a good example of Arts and Crafts architecture. Spring House, on the opposite side of the road, was the site of St James's National School from 1850 to 1968. Left of it there was once a fire station (firemen's cottages remain at the rear of the site). Almost opposite is Leaside Mansions, where firemen's helmets and axes are depicted on shields above the doors. Beyond are Twyford Court (1931) and Long Ridges (1930) both built by Collins. On the left-hand side is the 1904 Muswell Hill police station, and beyond it the Victorian Clissold Arms. Beyond it, Field Cottages are a reminder of the rural past, as are Coleraine Cottages and Fortis Green Cottages opposite the police station. Nos 4-7 Fortis Green Cottages at the rear of the Alexandra public house provide a rare example of back-to-back houses. The Alexandra (refaced in the 1930s) and Denmark Terrace beyond it on the right-hand side are a tribute to Princess Alexandra who in 1863 married the future Edward VII. Between them is Bomarsund which takes its name from a Crimean War incident and is a mid-nineteenth-century villa. An alley left of Denmark Terrace leads to Woodside Cottages, another nineteenth-century survivor.

Further along on this right-hand side is Albion Lodge, an attractive pair of listed 1830s houses set back from the road. Also listed are Nos 83-97 Fortis Green, a fine row of early nineteenth-century domestic properties. Fortis Green leads on to East Finchley, close to the tube station.

Sources and Reading List

Primary sources on which this book is based include historic maps, Hornsey Manor court rolls, various legal and sales documents, rate books, newspapers and directories, local authority reports and some unpublished studies, Secondary sources include church and institutional histories, articles in Hornsey Historical Society's annual printed bulletin and books relating to Muswell Hill and Hornsey published in the nineteenth and twentieth centuries.

   Those who wish to read further in local history are advised to contact the Hornsey Historical Society (136 Tottenham Lane, London N8 7EL; 020 8348 8429 – answerphone messages; www.hornseyhistorical.org. uk) which issues a publications list. This includes over two dozen titles dealing with local history, plus reproductions of historic maps and of historic postcards. The list includes details of *The Growth of Muswell Hill* by Jack Whitehead another account of the area. The following are not included in the list but are recommended to serious students:

Carrington, Ron, *Alexandra Park & Palace*, 1975.
Madge, S.J., *The Origin of the Name of Hornsey*, 1936.
The Early Records of Harringay alias Hornsey, 1938.
The Medieaval Records of Harringay alias Hornsey, 1939.
Richardson, John, *Highgate: Its History from the l5th Century*, 1983.
Robbins, Michael, *Middlesex*, 1953.
Travers, Ben, *The Book of Crouch End*, 1990.
Victoria County History of Middlesex, Volume VI, 1980.

Further illustrations, with captions, are to be found in three books published by The History Press:

Gay, Ken, *Hornsey & Crouch End*, reprinted 2008.
Schwitzer, Joan, & Ken Gay, *Highgate & Muswell Hill*, reprinted 2006.
Gay, Ken, *Muswell Hill Revisited*, 2009.

Index